Music
Business
Stories

By

Tom Cossie

STREET STUFF MUSIC
Publishing Books and Music

Dedicated to my granddaughter

Camryn

Born on my birthday January 13th

2008-2013

"One Heart" – "One Love"

Always…Pap

Table of Contents

A Time in Music

The 60's were a turning point in the world's music scene. Although the British invasion gets overwhelming credit for leading this music revolution, its roots were in working class America. While the Brits were reinterpreting American R&B, Americans were opening hundreds of independent labels across the country and finding interesting artists and songs of every description. The first Beatles U.S. releases were on indie labels Vee Jay and Swan. Elvis broke on Sun Records. These and hundreds of indies released tens of thousands of singles during the 50's and 60's. It was a time when 45 RPM singles outsold albums 20 to 1. These singles, retailing for 69 cents or less, along with thousands of "record hops" where DJs played records for teen audiences, drove new music discovery beyond anything that social networks powered by the internet and AI technology can offer.

Tom Cossie grew up in the heart of the exploding world of record collecting in the mid-sixties in Pittsburgh, Pennsylvania. His story is the story of how entrepreneurs, driven by a true love for music and music discovery, built an enormous global music industry. It is the story about how America was able to launch so many diverse hit recordings by so many artists. He had a presence that guided him beyond just wits and hustle to become a driving force in breaking so many hit songs and artists and play an important role in launching the disco genre.

His stories are an important archive for future generations and a warning from the past about why passion is more important than algorithms and profit. The book goes a long way to explain why the music streaming music "access" model has failed to break as many new artists as the old analog record ownership model along with record stores and small radio stations did prior to music and radio industry consolidation and the music technology revolution.

Each of us will draw a different lesson from his stories in this book. You will want to not just read it cover to cover as I did but keep it as a valuable archive to an era left behind and a man who believed himself to success.

Tom Silverman

Dance Music Report
New Music Seminar
TommY BoY Music

Acknowledgements

I will always remember their names and support they have given me over the decades:

From my days with Fenway and Hamburg Brothers Record Distributors: Herb Cohen, Nick Cenci, George Goodman, Elmer Willet, Fred Katz, Ray Anderson, Jack Hakim, Billy Roberts, Jay Cuniff, Joe Sulick, Murray Nagel, and Rosey.

From my days with RCA Records: Rocco Lagenestra, Dennis Katz, Augie Blume, Stan Montero, Judy Pearlmutter, Harry Kelleher, Harvey Cooper, Larry Douglass, Frank Mancini, Pat Kelleher, Joe Galante, Dominic Violini, Mike Spense, Roy Battocchio, Frank "Tookie" Dileo, Michael "The Rookie" Abramson, Don "Captain Spacy" Delacy, "Dandy Don" Whittemore, Ricki Renna, Tony "Teen Angel" Montgomery, Billy Bass, Bobby "The Z Man" Zurick, Bud "Stubby" Stebbins, Skip Pope, Andy Janis, Karen "Nancy Drew" Williams, Ray "Sweet Meat" Anderson, "Stu "The Jew" Ginsberg, Robb Hegal, Rochelle Greenblat, Ken Vandurant, David "Mag Man" Bupp, Chuck Dembrak, (My first employer and owner of Chuck's Record Shop), Elroy "Country Son" Kahanek, Long John Phillips, Kelvin Venture, Leroy Little,

Lou "Rocket Man" Galliani, Phil Rush, Steve Hahn, Steve Greenberg, Georgeann "Galante" Cifarelli, Al Mathias, Merlin Littlefield, Stu Sank, Tom "Drapes" Draper, Leroy Phillips, Carter "Cartier" Russel, Ray Harris, Nancy Pitts, Dorthy Difrancisco, Nick Sangiamo, Dorthy Steiner, Jack Mahar, Winston "Buzzy" Willis, Keith Jackson, Acy Lehman. Frank O'Donnell, Gene Settler, Mort Hoffman and Jack Kiernan.

From my days at Buddah Records: Art Kass, Bernie Sparago, Jude Lyons, Sylvia Rhone, Ed Goodgold, Billy Hendrex, Herb Rosen, Allan Lott, Jack Kreisberg, Dave Maney, Lewis Merenstein, Bill Browder, Milton Sincoff, Fred Rupert, Wade Conklin, Bob Perry, and Gary Bird

From my days with Atlantic and Big Tree Records: Ahmet Ertegun, Jerry Greenberg, Bobby Greenberg, Sheldon Vogel, Dick Krisman, George Furness, David Glew, Robert Defrin, Larry Yasgar, Dickie Klein, Vince Faraci, Simo Doe, Henry Allen, Doug Morris, Dick Vanderbilt, Dick Weber, Reene Nalli, and Topper Schroeder.

Yours truly,

Tommy "The Gentile" Cossie.

Music Business Stories

1950 to 1985

By: Tom Cossie

I've spent most of my life immersed in the music business, a journey filled with rhythm, reinvention, and remarkable people. Recently, I made the leap into authorship, a new chapter that feels less like a departure and more like natural progression. I used to view life in quarters, sports-style: four quarters, with some head-scratching over what exactly happened during halftime and a wary eye on the two-minute warning. These days, I lean more toward seeing life in thirds, like three acts or three periods in a game. Three periods feel more aligned with the tempo of a full, evolving life.

I often joke with friends that if I believed in reincarnation, and if I had a say in the matter, I'd come back as me. That's how lucky I feel, grateful to be alive, still curious, and still with stories worth sharing.

Over the past sixty years, I've been told more times than I can count, by friends and family, to write a book. "You've met so many fascinating and talented people," they'd say. "You've got to put this stuff down." Eventually, I listened.

After studying the memoirs from industry legends and book authors like: Ahmet Ertegun Clive Davis, and Rock Hall of Fame VP of Programming and Education David Spero, I decided: no ghostwriter and no recordings for translator interpretations. I wanted my stories to be told in my own unfiltered voice. With luck, I found a great editor named K. Adrian Zonneville, to help me polish the rough edges, and make me sound smarter and more well-read than I am. As he found out, that was no easy task.

Given the scope of my experiences, the companies I've been fortunate to be part of, and the wild, wonderful cast of characters I've encountered along the way, I chose to write this book from memory, and straight from the heart. My continued plan is to write a second book that continues to highlight the contributions of artists, the publication of a record industry magazine, managers, industry innovators, legal professionals, and colleagues who collectively influenced the evolution of the record business from 1986 to 2000. This subsequent collection will examine the development of *The R&B Report*, the establishment of Ear Candy Records, a collaboration with Nile Rodgers and BMG, the creation of Star Tracker Software, and the multifaceted experience of securing venture capital to build what was often referred to as, "a record company in a box."

FOREWARD

by Jack Forsythe

Among the many things the author of this book, Tom Cossie, and I have in common are our shared early-in-life love of music and love of a good true story. Not to mention we grew up in Pittsburgh and in music at a time when new music broke out of our region of the country. National large and small record label executives all paid strict attention to our region. I started out at 12 years old carrying sound equipment for Porky Chedwick (who Tom discusses in his early chapters) at local dances, then later I began DJing those dances. This led me to a career playing the local hits on the radio. Even though Tom and I worked for many of the same people that ran the local dance scene, it wasn't until my radio career that I first met Tom Cossie. We were both still young and eager to share great music with the world. I think it was immediate mutual respect and a genuine like of each other that anchored our friendship.

Tom would often visit the local pop, rock and R&B stations to introduce artists, solicit airplay, and, in general, solidify relationships with music programmers like me. Because he was from Pittsburgh, we were happy to spend more time with him than the other nationally known radio stations that he also had responsibility for. One of the funniest Pittsburgh 13Q visits happened a little later in his career. Tom brought his artist Andrea True, a porn star actress who's hit song "More, More, More" was topping the charts, to visit our studios on Stanwix Street in Pittsburgh. Later that evening several of our well-known DJs were embarrassingly seen by young listeners and their parents, with Andrea, leaving her movie that was playing in the red light theatre district of Pittsburgh. Not a place anyone wanted to be recognized. I'm sure you'll enjoy many of Tom's travel stories in this and later books.

As I moved around to other major market radio stations in cities like Miami and Jacksonville, Tom was always there with the latest and greatest music. I even admit here, based on our relationship, I played a few records for him that were not good enough to really be hits for us.

Later, as the years went by, I watched Tom's career and keen love of music take him to the heights of the industry itself. In my time running the National Charts out of Los Angeles it was fun to often visit Tom in New York or get together in L. A. to regale many of the fantastic stories Tom shares here with you, his readers, in this biography.

"Music is an agreeable harmony for the honor of God and the permissible delights of the soul." — Johann Sebastian Bach

For me music is truly a religious experience. Maybe my days as lead choirboy in grade school is the reason, church music still moves me emotionally but so then does any great song. I realized early in my career there were a few different kinds of folks you would meet in the music business:

*In it for the ego/prestige

*In it for the money

*In it and didn't know why

*And then there were the few in it for the love of music

Tom had prestige, he made money, but he knew why he was in the record business, and it was indeed for the love of music. That was the strongest bond we shared as it was at the core of who we were. That was his motivation. I've always believed that passion and authenticity are magnets for success, and success was Tom when it came to representing or signing great artists to a record label, and then getting the hits played on radio. It's the early years of a career and the (hopefully) expert people you meet early that decides the high standards for goals set and achieved. Here, we were blessed with those kinds of mentoring professionals.

Tom was one of the music execs I tried to fashion myself after when I became Vice President at Chrysalis Records. I think some of my Chrysalis artists Pat Benatar, Huey Lewis, and Billy Idol would agree that the "authentic" secret sauce worked well. Tom mentored many folks in the business and probably even didn't realize he was mentoring, but folks who simply followed his example.

Reading through Tom's book about his amazing career, all in a time that pop music was climbing to its pinnacle in history, leads me to tell you, the completed series of his career will be a great inside look at 4 decades of Tom's work life. The overview of music from the 60's, 70's, 80's and 90's will delight music enthusiasts and gives a case study in the evolution of change in the record industry. Additionally meeting some of the non-famous people/characters he introduces you to, are the people that helped bring those artists to national and international acclaim. This is guaranteed to be entertaining, funny, and enjoyable. The stories are fascinating and true. These stories will bring back heartfelt mental sounds, "Ear Candy", memories for everyone.

Sit back with a choice beverage and enjoy the storied ride down memory lane in the lives of your favorite artists, music and hit songs from days long gone but not yet forgotten

Chapter One

Early Pittsburgh Days

My parents, Jim and Louise Surman, reared our family in a small steel town in Western Pennsylvania just outside of Pittsburgh, called Munhall. Louise Tyke grew up in Lincoln Place, an equally small town just two miles further up the trolley tracks. She attended Taylor Alderdice High School, was the first seat cellist in their orchestra and an art student. My Dad, Jim, grew up in the city of Pittsburgh, near the Heinz House. He was a trumpet player and tenor vocalist with his band, The Polish Aristocrats. Louise later joined my dad's band, playing on the road for a few years before starting a family which produced five children: Jimmy, Chuckie, Tommy, Tony, and Louise. This story is about the one in the middle, Yours Truly, Tommy.

In 1952, Jim and Louise established an appliance store on Main Street in Munhall. My father had a keen interest in the technology of that time, and his store featured the latest televisions, radios, and appliances available. The storefront at 3614 Main Street was constructed as an addition to a modest three-bedroom, one- bathroom Insu brick home. I was five years old and remember peering between phonographs and radios through the large showroom window watching the number 65 steel wheeled trolley roll by. We called those big red and white metal cylinders, powered by overhead electric lines, "streetcars." They rumbled down Main Street on steel tracks, ringing a crisp bell as they went from Lincoln Place to Homestead. My two older brothers and I would place rolls of caps on the tracks, then hide behind the bushes, waiting for the 65 to pass. The train's wheels grinding on the metal tracks would ignite the caps, creating a sequential series of explosive bangs.

It's amazing how siblings, born from the same parents and reared under the same household could be so different. Brother Jimmy was the oldest and seven years my senior, and Brother Chuckie was five years older than me. The difference between them was drastic. Jimmy's bike had no chain guard, no rear fender, or handle grips and a brush painted frame of robin egg blue. His bike did have a front fender with a chrome devil's head ornament attached, its thumb to its nose, and four fingers pointing to the sky. Chuckie's bike was a Schwinn Roadmaster, cream and green, full fenders, fully dressed, chrome mirrors, a horn and headlight. His bike was always kept in pristine condition. Their personalities reflected their bikes. Jimmy was James Dean reincarnate, had a small collection of Playboy magazines, and earned money by hustling pool for fun and profit. Chuckie's library contained books with schematics for building model airplanes and shortwave radios. He was very frugal, saved all his earnings and kept his cash in a cigar box under his bed. I thought for sure Jimmy would turn out to be a cowboy or numbers runner, and Chuckie, a buttoned-down scientist or engineer. I was right about Chuckie. However, Jimmy changed his ways after marrying a beautiful Italian girl, AnnaJean Sinatra, he went to college and became an efficiency expert in corporate America consulting hospitals.

My parents' store, Surman Electric, was the pioneering establishment in the city for retailing and servicing televisions. The showroom featured models from DuMont, Zenith, and RCA, alongside refrigerators and Electrolux vacuum cleaners, including both upright and canister models. Additionally, the store offered the latest console cabinet radios and record players.
During that period, news and sports were predominantly broadcast via radio. Despite being only five years old at the time, I retain clear memories of that era, 73 years ago.

The DuMont TVs and early RCA black-and-white screens were especially popular. The screens were no larger than 12 inches, and when you removed the back cover of a TV, you would see a large picture tube in the center, surrounded by smaller tubes. Customers often returned for service when their TV's picture or sound went out, a common occurrence back then. My dad accused me of being the most "nebby" of his kids, though I knew he just meant, extremely inquisitive, as I would watch intently as he repaired the defective appliances.

He taught me how to use a large machine called a tube tester. I was in second grade, six years old, and operating that space-age-looking device. Customers marveled at seeing this little kid confidently diagnosing faulty tubes. When customers came in saying, "The picture went out," I would say, "It's probably a 5U4 GT, or "I have picture but no sound, I would say, most likely a 6SN7." I listened closely to my dad's explanations. I knew how to identify tube failure. I could plug the tubes into the tester, dial the settings, and push a few buttons. A needle on the screen would then indicate whether the tube was good (green) or bad (red). It wasn't a difficult process, but to our customers, watching a child operate this daunting-looking device was fascinating.

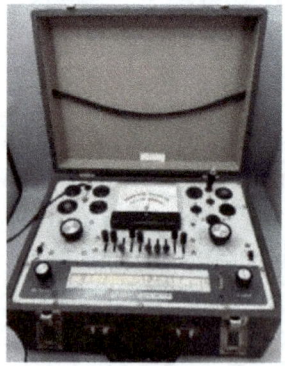 

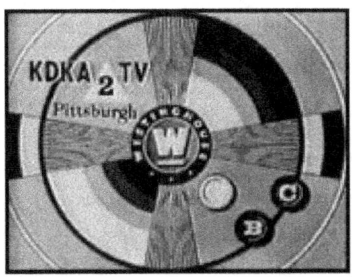

I entered Park Elementary school as a 5-year-old first grader. Back then if you turned five by January you could enter first grade. I remember walking to school about a half a mile away, also located on Main Street. Everything important seemed to happen on Main Street. I was the youngest and second tallest in my first grade class. Second grade at Park would become my last year in public elementary school.

Aside from testing tubes and nursing a crush on my first-grade heart throb, Becky Blevins, I had other memorable experiences that year. I would buy Lucky Strike cigarettes for my dad at Gracie's convenience store, located directly across from Park School. Three times a week I was armed with a note from my dad and a quarter. Grace was a pleasingly plumb and jovial older woman, after a few weeks of familiarity, the note was no longer needed. I would hand her the quarter, receive the pack of Lucky Strikes and a nickel and penny change, I'd spend the penny on a long piece of black shoestring licorice and when I got home, give my dad his cigarettes and a nickel change. One day, trying to be cool got the better of me.

I decided to try one of those unfiltered Lucky Strikes. I figured dad wouldn't notice one missing. Hiding behind some trees on my walk back home, I lit up and inhaled taking a long hard drag. My chocking episode did not go unnoticed. My two brothers were riding their bikes and saw me, started laughing, and hurriedly pumped their bikes back home. They arrived five minutes ahead of me. I was positive they were going to rat me out. Chuckie told our dad he saw the whole thing, Jimmy said he saw nothing, and my dad saw a second grader with a red and green complexion. The result of my adult moment was I felt so sick that I never touched another cigarette again. That is until college, where, once again, I lit up, but this time to look cool while playing poker, with a luger dangling from my lip for effect.

My parents expanded our family, adding two new family members, Tony and Louise, then decided to sell the store as more room was needed for our growing family. We moved across the street into a larger home. As good Catholics, and with a new school and church opening only six blocks away on Main Street, my parents made it imperative I attend, and so I did through eighth grade.

At the age of seven and in third grade, I became an altar boy and had to learn the Mass in Latin. *'Ad Deum Qui Laetificat Juventutem Meam'*, meaning, 'To the God Who Gives Joy to My Youth'. How apropos at age seven. Learning Latin or any foreign language was a lot easier when you were in those young formative years. I memorized the entire mass in a few weeks. Seventy plus years later, I've been trying to learn Spanish, and for the past four years I finally mastered one word, Hola.

The nuns adored me because I was the only one who would willingly serve the 5 a.m. Mass at the convent. Sister Mary Clifford was my favorite nun, and our grade school principal. Many times, I would be the only altar boy who showed up, so we became fast friends. She was also the organizer and scheduler for all the Mass servers. One of my duties before each Mass was to fill the cruets with wine and water. I think my passion for wine dates to those days preparing the cruets for Mass. I was an altar boy for five years.

Upon entering seventh grade I needed to make some money, so I had to restructure my priorities, with two new kids at home, everything other than food was a luxury. That year, I took over a paper route from one of my brother's friends. The route covered 96 customers over a 20-block radius and consisted of delivering and collecting the money each week for two newspapers: The Daily Messenger and The Pittsburgh Press. Sundays were the toughest, with bulky editions stuffed with supplements and ads. Every Sunday at 4 a.m., I would assemble 130 Sunday Edition Pittsburgh Press papers and load them for delivery. The process involved three large loads of one-inch-thick Sunday papers, using my Red Rider Wagon with extended side panels. I started the first delivery at 5:30 a.m. and finished the third wagon load by 11:00 a.m., allowing me time to make the noon Sunday Mass service.

I loved the work, earning $15 a week plus tips. As an 11-year-old I was flush with cash. I knew if I put the paper in the customers door when it was raining or snowing, I would get an extra dime or quarter at the end of each week. Christmas season tips were a special financial highlight.

It was my responsibility to both deliver and collect every Friday. As a kid I learned the value of time and money. On a normal day I would deliver 75 Press and 60 Daily Messengers and would complete my run in an hour and a half. Fridays were long days. I would deliver and collect payments from over 100 customers. It would take me five hours and often I would have to revisit the next morning if the people weren't home. Late Saturday afternoon, I would meet my route manager, Mr. Rege, and pay him for the week. If customers didn't pay me, I was still responsible to pay the route man. By the time I graduated eighth grade, my two-year newspaper delivery career was over.

During that time, my mom said I grew over a foot and gained thirty pounds. I learned that making money requires working both hard and smart. Dealing with the public was often challenging, and my dad would always tell me; "The customer is always right, except when they don't pay".

As a high school freshman, instead of enrolling in the local public high school, Munhall High, I decided I wanted to be a priest and enter the Seminary. I knew all the priests from my time as an altar boy and thought being a priest could be a cool job. Though priests were not snappy dressers, only wearing black, the upside was they did have some cool looking newer cars. Perhaps my priestly calling was the allure of sampling wine as an altar boy, or maybe I just liked the idea of telling the nuns I had a priestly vocation in mind. That attitude in Catholic grade school always had a positive effect on the grading curve.

Bishop Wright, the Pittsburgh Diocesan Bishop, had begun a pre-seminary program in downtown Pittsburgh. Classes were held at Epiphany Church and grade school, located at the base of the Hill District. I knew this downtown landmark because my dad would take me to Epiphany once a month. In addition to owning an appliance store, as mentioned, my dad was an amazing tenor vocalist and trumpet player.

Epiphany was a traditional Pittsburgh Catholic Church with a large choir loft in back facing the alter. I remember walking up two flights of old wooden stairs into a large open room where I watched my dad sing the Mass in Latin, accompanied by an organist. He always sang at the 12:00 noon Mass, which was moderately attended by diehards who loved the traditional Latin service.

My dad once told me, "The Mass service with

the largest attendance was the 2:30 a.m. Sunday morning Mass.

I told him I thought that getting up to serve Mass at the convent at 5:00 was early and couldn't believe people actually got up that early to go to church.

He replied, "Those people didn't just wake up, they just rolled out of the bars after last call for alcohol. They would then head directly over to Epiphany for this special mass which would fulfill their Sunday obligation."

I thought to myself, 'and they say the Catholic Church isn't flexible. Here they were always willing to serve the needs of even the late-night worshipers.'

Attending my high school freshman year at a Jesuit Seminary, exposed me to a world of enriched experiences: luncheons, art galleries, Broadway performances at the Playhouse in Oakland, and advanced academic classes. After this enlightening experience, the next three years in a public high school would prove to be culturally anticlimactic. After one year in Bishop Wrights minor seminary, I had the option to continue at St. Gregory's in Indiana, as a full-time seminarian. At this point I decided I did not have the vocation in becoming a priest.

As I look back, I think I would have become a great priest, or Bishop, or Cardinal, and maybe even a shot at the Conclave. After 58 years of marriage, I often share at parties how my wife swept me off my feet and diverted me from becoming a man of the cloth. A fabrication that would assuredly make her roll her eyes since we didn't meet for another few years. I do, however, blame my priesthood exit on my brother Jimmy's collection of Playboy and similar thought-provoking magazines.

High School and a Vinyl Future

Public school it was, I enrolled in Munhall High School, grades 10 through 12. The school was just three blocks from the main entrance of The Homestead Steel Works. Munhall's streets were interwoven with those of Homestead, so depending on where you stood, you were steps away from being in either town. Homestead was once the center and Steel Capitol of the World. Steel was synonymous with Pittsburgh, The Steel City, and The Pittsburgh Steelers. Like most booming mill towns back then, employment was 100% and almost everyone wanted to or would end up working for US Steel. Legendary steel plants and machine shops dotting the banks of the Monongahela River with; The Irwin Works, The Baddock Works, and The Homestead Works. US Steel dominated many miles along the Monongahela waterfront into Downtown Pittsburgh.

This steel city would be known as the largest mill town in the world, rolling out millions of tons of Steel. Our riverbanks were so packed with rolling mills and crucibles pouring melted steel, some nights the skies would glow from the slag dumps as trains would pour red hot spent steel molds down the sides of the tops of large slag mountains in Pittsburgh's South Hills.

As a typical mill town, Homestead had plenty of bars, churches, coffee shops, clothing stores, pharmacies with soda fountains, pool halls, and at least one classic movie theatre. Eighth Avenue in Homestead also had two record stores, Chuck's and Kuban's. The town additionally had an upscale restaurant, by Homestead standards, called Buffington's. On the corner of 8th Ave. and the High Level Bridge, was the location and home of Pittsburgh's number one R&B radio station, WAMO.

No matter the area where you grew up in our country, there would always be stories of a celebrity or two who made their way to the top. My hometown area was no exception. It so happened, my mother's dentist, Doctor Goldblum, had a famous movie star son named Jeff, who was featured in movies like: *Wicked, Jurassic Park and Independence Day*, and like his father and my mom, they all had attended Taylor Allderdice high school. I'm told the billionaire owner of sports teams, and one of the stars of Shark Tank, Mark Cuban, grew up a few miles downriver from Homestead in Hazelwood.

Michael Keaton was also a Pittsburgh Yinzer, and movie star in: *Beetlejuice, Bat Man, Johnnie Dangerously,* and, more importantly, a member of the Pittsburgh famous, low wire/no net performing act, "The Flying Zookini's".

During my days in high school, I began collecting 45 rpm records, with a particular love for Rhythm and Blues (R&B), and records with a dance beat. My high school nickname was "Cosmo," which was later shortened to "Cos" and eventually "Cossie." This name originated from the character Cosmo from the Beetle Bailey comic strip. My friends somehow made the association.

While in high school I worked at one of the record stores. After classes I would walk from Munhall High School to Chuck's Record Shop, wait on customers, check in orders, and sort records in Chuck's upstairs storage area. One block away from Chuck's was WAMO, one of the hottest R&B stations in the country. Porky Chedwick, was the AM radio station's drive time jock, and one of the most popular Disc Jockeys in the area. He identified himself on the station as: "The Boss Man" or "The Platter-Pushing Poppa," and "Pork the Tork" and sometimes say, "It's not George Washington...It's Pork Torkington." He would play a mixture of newly released R&B music, that was often months ahead of the national charts, as well as older, more obscure Rhythm and Blues 45's.

Porky and fans at the Bi -Centennial Picnic.
Photo by Michael Valentine Smith

Porky was an influencer rather than a follower when it came to music trends. As an R&B enthusiast and record collector, I was one of his biggest fans.

Chapter Two

Roots in Records and Radio

Every major city in the USA had its own unique or controversial radio DJ's who played their own music of choice in the 50's and 60's. Payola was prevalent and became front page news in the mid 1950's and early 1960's. The dawn of the 45 rpm single made it possible for hundreds of new releases to hit the market on a weekly basis. Competition became elevated regarding getting records played on radio and a quick way to get a record played was to pay off a DJ, not only to add your record, but to play your song before and more often than others released. The government stepped in regarding fair trade practices and went after radio jocks like Cleveland's well-known DJ, Alan Freed, as well as TV's well known music host, Dick Clark. Freed was fired from radio and Dick Clark avoided payola charges by divesting himself from interests he owned in the industry. In the late 1960's radio changed course, and individual jocks' played music being added and programmed by a radio station's music director, and/or program director. Jocks then had to play only the records programed on their radio stations playlist. Drawing a contrast from those pay to play practices, Porky while on WAMO, never accepted

"Payola" to play records. Porky's sole criteria for playing a record was, did the music meet his standard of "being in the grooves."

Clark Race was another popular afternoon drive time radio personality on the 50,000-watt powerhouse KDKA-AM. This radio signal not only covered the Pittsburgh listening audience and most of Pennsylvania but also could be heard in six additional states. Clark Race, like Porky, was given free rein on what he wanted to play and often ended up playing a lot of the records my collector friends and I were playing in our dance clubs. This great variety of music made it fun listening to the radio in the late 50's and mid 60's. Rege Cordic became the KDKA morning show personality with entertaining skits like promoting a make-believe beer called 'Olde Frothing Slosh, 'the beer with the foam on the bottom'. Jack Bogut, another great radio personality, followed Rege in the morning slot for the next 15 years. Both of those morning drive jocks mellowed out with their music programming when KDKA became a bit more conservative in their choice of music. My reasoning for this format change was they started airing Pirate Baseball, and their target demographic changed, their music programming choice followed suit catering to an older audience.

During my teenage years and early twenties, my record collection included approximately 5,000 Rock & Roll, and Rhythm and Blues 45 rpm records, most of which were obscure. Obscure meaning only a handful of those records were currently popular or on any radio station chart. They were older undiscovered releases that I thought were great, and as a DJ, worthy of being played at my dances. I would research the history of the artists and in doing so developed a deep knowledge of the record labels as well as the artists they represented. The NYC based Atlantic Records was one of my favorite collectable labels, yellow and black Atlantic labels to be specific. Chess Records out of Chicago also had a lot of great soulful artists and were also a great label to collect.

'For Your Precious Love' by Jerry Butler was one of my favorites. I knew the history and owners of Atlantic as well as the artists and history of many other record labels like: Roulette, Checker, Imperial, Argo, End, Gone, Ace, Rust, and Hull. There were nationally released groups and solo artists which only received airplay in clubs and boutique radio stations in Pittsburgh. Though some of these records were recently released, they were still referred to as "oldies but goodies". 'My Heart Cries' by Billy Vera and the Contrasts, 'A Penny For Your Thoughts' by Bruce Clark and the Q's, 'Jimmy Lee' by The Jewels, 'Monkey Man' by Baby Huey and the Babysitters, and 'High on a Hill' by Scott English, were some of the must have singles in every Pittsburgh record collector and club DJ's record collections. The owners and promotion heads of the labels would visit our city on a regular basis.

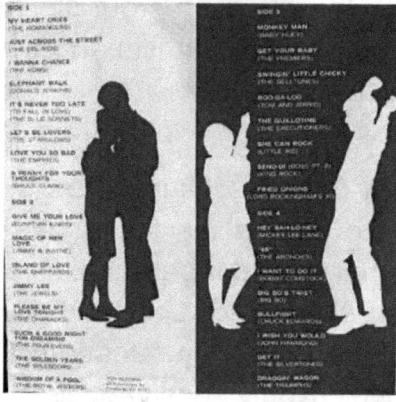

Pittsburgh's Greatest Hits, complements of Travis Klein

Pittsburgh back then was considered one of several breakout markets in the USA for R&B and Pop music. During my sophomore year in college, I earned a third-class radio license and had a radio show on WESA located near the college. I played records at dance clubs like The Blue Fox in Monongahela and The White Elephant in McKeesport. Those opportunities provided insight into music trends and popularity with the record-buying public. Our dance clubs from the late 60's paved the way for the elaborate discos of the late 70's like Studio 54. I also played records for Porky, Terry Lee, and Bob Mac, at their venues. We were all confident in our knowledge of the music scene and played new unproven artists and unique records from our collections. This was a great time, to hear a broad spectrum of new music, break new artists, and to be in the business we loved, The Music Business.

Porky was really *"The* Boss *Man''* when it came to playing dance and R&B music. R&B music was the true roots of Rock & Roll. Music from artists like: Chuck Berry, Bo Diddley, Little Richard, The Dells, Jerry Butler, The Coasters, The Clovers, The Flamingos, Billy Ward and the Domino's, and Harvey and the Moonglows, as well as numerous Gospel artists, paved the musical direction for Elvis, Bill Haley and the Comets, The Beatles, and Rolling Stones.

During the 60's and 70's rhythmic tunes and two-step dance ballads were the music of choice for high school and college aged kids. The greater Pittsburgh area had its fair share of key dance clubs that played and supported the music. Our dance halls were the go-to entertainment destinations throughout Western PA and the borders of Ohio and West Virginia. Ohio and West Virgina dance halls were more popular since the drinking age was 18. My fellow record collector/disc jockeys: Ronnie the OZ, Franco Da Banko Spelic, The Squid, The Rat, Lightning, Bill

Zimp Zimpleman, The Harv, Louie Rizzuto, Freddy Bond, Richie Antoncic, Bill Kabumsky Kaminsky, Skippy Smith, Bob Lavorio, Big Jim Engle, Beans, Bobby Z, Mad Mike, Bob Mack and TL were all serious record collectors and club DJ's who knew their music. Bob Mack, TL "Terry Lee" and Mad Mike also were top radio DJ's playing their own exclusive music from their record collections. Terry had a prominent radio show called "Music for Young Lovers" which broadcasted out of McKeesport on WMCK.

Mike's show was called "Mad Mikes Moldies", and Bob Mack was "The Geeter with the Heater", both men had radio shows airing on WZUM.

Mad Mike was by far the most eccentric and extremely possessed record collector in the city. Though I thought I was the "Cool One" with a robust record collection of over 5,000 45 rpm records. I was riding high until I found out that Mad Mike had close to 50,000 45's in his collection. Mike even rented a home just to store some of his records. His collection consisted of an abundant array of titles, along with some quantity of each title. When Mike discovered a record he liked, most of which never made the radio charts, he would buy as many as he could. He would play his Mad Mike Exclusives, create a demand, then sell off a few copies to other record collectors, but not before he ripped off the record labels. He did so to protect the records' identity and therefore maintained his exclusivity. Mike would then bury the remaining copies at his record storage home. Cool plan, but a little too unfulfilling to me as a devoted fan of capitalism. Many dollar opportunities were left on the table, or in Mike's case buried in his basement.

Looking back, I guess I was never a true record collector, but more of a record speculator. When I played one of my exclusives at my dances and created a demand, if I had ten copies, I would sell nine to the highest bidders. If the record really became popular, I would track down the source of ownership and try to corner the market on as many copies as I could find. There were also some scoundrels who would bootleg the record, that is, make unauthorized pressings, provided there was a big enough demand. Every record I owned had a price. Those records paid for my college education, an engagement ring, a car, my parents' cars and many great lunches and dinners. Just about every member in our collector's group were purest collectors who hoarded their 45 rpm records. Only Bobby Z and I were the mercenaries willing to sell our 45's, including the carrying cases, for the right price.

Pittsburgh's inner city and suburbs had noteworthy dance clubs. The Lebanon Lodge in Mt. Lebanon, White Elephant, McKeesport, Bethel Park Arena, Red Rooster in Greensburg, The Blue Fox in Monongahela, Westview Dance Land, The Terena in Tarentum, The Grove, and the Jolly Green Giant in the South Hills were just some of the hot spots. These clubs were not gymnasium-looking facilities; more so, they resembled some of the more sophisticated dance clubs you see today. Raised dance floors, killer sound systems, multiple high-end turntables for mixing records, and stages with great lighting. Artists' careers were launched from the airplay and exposure from those clubs.

'Hanky Panky' by Tommy James and the Shondells was one such record and artist. His single was only a few years old, and on a small one artist label out of Niles, Michigan, Snap Records. Tommy James and the Shondells story began in that small town, and years later took an eventful and positive detour through Pittsburgh, launching his career.

As a record collector along with a multitude of other collectors in Pittsburgh, I would find cool but obscure 45's in any discount store that sold overstocked products and promo records. One key prospect for these treasures was five-and-dime discount stores like Kresge's and Murphy's. Those stores carried a little of everything, including an abundance of all those unwanted 45's that never make it on the radio stations' airwaves. Our record collector group regularly visited those stores, searching through hundreds of obscure records for interesting titles. The price was 10 for $1.00. Popular 45's with radio play back then sold for $.69 cents a record. The chance was, when you bought those ten cent specials, you might find one or two out of the batch that sounded good, the rest just had good sounding titles. 'Hanky Panky' was one of those with both an interesting title and also happened to sound great. We started playing that single at all the dance clubs and the kids went crazy over *'Hanky Panky'*. The record became an overnight local hit. Club owner and DJ, Bob Mack, brought Tommy James to Pittsburgh to perform at four of his clubs. The demand for the record was so large that someone, not to be named, bootlegged close to 40,000 *'Hanky Panky'* singles on the original label, Snap records. The sales figures were amazing for an unknown artist. Activity in clubs and on local radio led to national attention.

Bob Mack, being an entrepreneur, club owner, and promoter, signed Tommy to Morris Levy's Roulette Records in NYC. Shortly thereafter, the record went Gold. One must wonder how many artists like Tommy James and records like *'Hanky Panky'* are out there waiting to be discovered but will never see the light of day. I learned early on, an artist or song can be great, but without being in the right place, at the right time, and having the proper promotion, connections, and marketing, nothing will happen.

I remember driving Tommy to The White Elephant in 1965, one of Bob Mack's clubs in McKeesport. Tommy told me, "This is the beginning, it's my destiny to be a hit artist," I said "Yeah, and I think it's my destiny that someday I'm going to own my own major record label." Tommy James was 100% correct and had numerous hit records: *'I Think We're Alone Now'*, *'Crystal Blue Persuasion'*, *'Mony Mony'*, and

'*Crimson and Clover*'. Tommy Cossie, on the other hand, was only about 70% correct and became a Senior VP at RCA at age 26, would launch a not so big but nationally distributed record label, Saturn Records, and would become the publisher of a national trade magazine, The R&B Report.

Buried Warehouse Gold

You may be wondering where those bargain store treasured 45 RPM records came from? Then again, you may not be wondering at all, however, I'm going to tell the story anyway.

One winter day back in 1964 I was making my weekly discount store, record hunting trip, and ran into a large gruff looking guy who appeared to be a little older than me. We were collectively rummaging through a large bin of 45 rpm records, and I opened the conversation by saying, "I wonder who supplies all the records to these stores". He smiled and introduced himself as Jim Engel. He stated he was not sure, but confirmed the stores received a fresh supply every Thursday. Jim told me he was a sophomore at Youngstown University, and he had found these discount record bins everywhere. I looked under the display area holding the records and saw several labeled boxes with a shipping address from Galgano's One-Stop, Armitage Ave. Chicago Ill. Having keen sense of the obvious, I said, "I bet this is their supplier", and showed Jim the shipping carton label.

Jim and I became fast friends. Every Saturday he would visit Chuck's Record Shop in Homestead. We'd trade records and grab a beer at a popular local tavern a few storefronts away.

I was 17, Jim was 20, but back then the laws were a bit looser regarding the drinking age, especially in bars along the river valley. On one Saturday afternoon, Jim and I were having fish sandwiches and fishbowl drafts at our favorite Homestead tavern, when my dad walked in and sat directly across the bar from us. I told Jim, 'Oh Crap, that's my dad.' My dad looked over, studied us both for a few seconds then told the bartender, "Give those guys each a hard-boiled egg and a few drafts on me." Those hard-boiled eggs were located in a large glass jar, submerged in some sort of yellow/gold preservative liquid. They were, believe it or not, a big bar item back then. Without hesitation, my dad raised his glass and said, "Cheers guys! Tommy, who's your large friend?"

During those strategic bar meetings with Big Jim Engel, we laid out our plans to make the road trip to Chicago and check out Galgano's. I did my research and found out Tony Galgano owned the operation, and it was run by his son Johnny. I discovered that independent distributors nationwide would unload their excess inventory and leftover promotional records to places like Galgano's. Galgano's would then create packages called Bag O' Tunes with 5 records in a package for 50 cents or just sell unpackaged bulk quantities of 45's across the country to discount department stores and the five and dime stores.

The following day, I located the phone number for Galgano's and contacted Johnny. I informed him that I had record stores in Pittsburgh and could supply a bulk quantity of 45's at three cents per record. The records would be new, including some stock and some DJ copies. It was necessary to specify new records because jukebox operators occasionally attempted to sell their heavily used records to warehouses like Galgano's, which included scratches and hiss. Johnny expressed interest, provided that the batch included some recognizable artists.

Over the years, Chuck's Record Shop bought out smaller distributors who went out of business. He had thousands of 45's in storage and I knew Chuck was anxious to clean out his second-floor storage area. Jim and I cut a deal with Chuck to take everything and in return give him some of our newly acquired goods upon our return. The plan was to take Chuck's records and trade them for some of the products we would find at Galgano's. Chuck gave us seventy 100 count boxes of those 45's. I calculated 7,000 records at three cents each would only net us $210.00. Jim and I had the idea that once we got to Galgano's, we would not take the money but trade records and give Galgano's three records for everyone we wanted. They didn't seem to care what the records were as long as there were recognizable songs and at least contained some well-known artists. We wanted the opposite, the more obscure the records the better. Now we needed to find a vehicle to make the 9 hour trip from Pittsburgh to Chicago. I asked Jim if he knew anybody who could lend us a large car or small truck and if that person would be willing to accept records as payment in exchange for the service. Jim immediately said, "Mad Mike". He knew Mike had multiple vehicles and would probably lend us one of his cars if we gave him the first choice of the records we brought back.

Mike's taste in cars, like his taste in records, was eccentric. All his cars were at least ten years old, and mostly in average condition. Among the vehicles in Mad Mike's fleet, was a 1956 Chrysler 300. We checked it out and felt it was the only one capable of making the journey both ways. It was also the only one whose trunk and back seat would accommodate the quantity and weight of approximately 7,000 45 rpm records. On the flipside that model Chrysler had a Hemi V8 engine and got about 6 miles to the gallon on the highway.

It was early Sunday evening when we began the journey, planning on driving all night to arrive at Galgano's' early Monday morning. Earlier that afternoon, we'd loaded Mike's Chrysler. When we pulled out of Homestead, Jim said he had to make a quick stop to his Youngstown apartment.

He needed to work out some small problem with his live-in girlfriend and pick up some clean shirts. We arrived at his apartment on a cool summer's evening to find his third-floor apartment window open and all his clothing, among other household items, strewn about the front lawn. Apparently, that small girlfriend problem was not so small after all. Jim walked up three flights of stairs to his apartment only to find the door locked and bolted from inside. Without hesitation, he returned to the car, pausing briefly to collect a few items from the front lawn and we were off to Chicago.

During our journey to Galgano's, we made three stops, two to refuel. The third stop was in Gary, Indiana, located just outside of Chicago. We still had a half tank of gas, so this stop was not because of being low on gas. As I looked out of the rearview mirror, I noticed a stream of blue smoke coming from behind the car. Fortunately, we were only two miles from the Gary service area. We stopped; I opened the hood to find smoke billowing off the manifold. There was a slight gas leak coming from a rubber fuel line and gas was dripping on the exhaust manifold causing the built-up oil and grease to smoke. A small fire had broken out and some of the wiring also caught fire. I had to use my jacket to smother the flames. As we let the car cool down, we found a small roll of electric tape in Mike's glove box. I taped the two compromised spark plug wires as well as the leaking rubber carburetor fuel line. We topped the tank and were on our way limping slowly to our destination on Armitage Avenue.

We arrived mid-morning after a 12-hour journey and parked at Galgano's warehouse loading dock. Johnny Galgano came out, looked through several of the boxes and said, "ok, you got it, three cents a record."

I replied, "Rather than giving us cash, we would like to look at the inventory you ship to your discount stores. If we can check some boxes in your warehouse, we will give you three records for each one we take. We will take a full 100-count box of each selection along with any smaller quantities laying around."

We thought this was a good sales pitch, instead of taking only one or two 45's from each box, we would take the entire box. No cash would need to change hands. Johnny also thought that was a fair deal. We grabbed two large carts from his warehouse and started to unload our shipment onto the loading dock. After the unloading process I had to move the car. I have to admit, because of the fire, I was a bit concerned, but it started, so I moved it out front, across the street from the entrance to Galgano's. The location happened to be in front of a used car lot. After three days of foraging through countless boxes of records, and two glorious nights staying at a local YMCA, we had set aside close to two thousand records. We were extremely happy with our mission, selecting quantities of cool titles and smaller numbers of hard-to-get older titles as well. One of our findings included a 100-count box of 'Hanky Panky' by Tommy James and The Shondells. A title that was already getting exclusive airplay in our clubs.

As luck would have it, the owner of the car lot across the street called his friend, Johnny Galgano, and asked if he knew who owned the Chrysler 300 parked in front of his lot. Moments later Jim and I walked over, and the owner of the used car lot asked if we would be interested in selling him that somewhat beautiful, slightly used Chrysler 300. We both simultaneously said yes. We did, however, explain the wiring and gas line repair, but the car started and didn't sound too out of tune. Johnny told his car dealer friend we were trustworthy, and the dealer gave us two hundred dollars cash with the promise of the title to be signed and sent to him from Mad Mike. The money paid for a small one-way truck rental and our expenses back to Pittsburgh.

Upon our return, Mike told us he was surprised the car made it one way to Chicago and was thrilled to have his pick off the top of our find. Mike took close to 300 records. Most of his selections came from our small batch record find. Mike told us several of the records he took were on the SARG label and were worth more than his car. Chuck, who gave us the records to trade, was equally satisfied receiving almost seven hundred records, all of which he planned on selling for between $2.00 and $5.00 a copy. Jim and I divvied up the rest and made our own deals selling exclusives to other record collectors and people who attended our dances. We sold our copies of *Hanky Panky* with the label intact. Which was now an ideal candidate for bootlegging, which, as I mentioned earlier, did happen. To the benefit of Tommy James and his recording career.

Chapter Three

Record Distribution Evolution

The late 60's and early 7O's were considered by many to be a Golden Age in the record industry as well as a time of great political and social upheaval. The new artists in the music scene were Rod Stewart and the Faces, Three Dog Night, Credence Clearwater Revival, Led Zeppelin, and many more. Smoking a dooby was commonplace as well as political activism. Crosby, Stills, Nash, and Young harmonized about Kent State in protest of the Vietnam war.

Meanwhile independent record distributors were streamlined into a path of direct distribution, which created the major record labels of the day and set the record industry model into motion for the next four decades. In the early 60's, there were over 250 independent record distributors and one-stops around the country in both primary and secondary markets. Each independent distributor carried specific labels and lines of products sold to record stores. The One Stop was a wholesale outlet that denotes just that, one stop shopping. A small mom and pop store could pay a few extra pennies per record just for the convenience of having to make only one stop while picking up all the releases they needed from one place.

During this time, the major independent distributors across the country were Fenway and Hamburg Brothers in Pittsburgh, Universal in Philadelphia, Mainline and Record Rendezvous in Cleveland, MS in Chicago, Hotline in Memphis, Big State in Texas, Heilicher in Miami, and California Records and Tapes on the west coast. These were a few of the key distributors which carried many of the major label manufacturers as well as the smaller independent record labels. When the transition to direct distribution took place in the late 60's, most of the larger record labels including Motown, (Motown, Tamala, Gordy), RCA, Warner (which later became Warner Electra Atlantic), Columbia Epic (which later became CBS), and ABC Dunhill opted for direct distribution to serve all retail outlets.

There were several compelling reasons for this transition from independent distribution to direct distribution; however, not every label jumped onto the direct distribution mode of operation. A lot of the smaller labels did not have the infrastructure to make the jump on their own. However, the larger labels had figured out by cutting out the middleman, the independent distributors, and selling direct to retailers, the results would mean greater profit margins and provide exclusive control in prioritizing releases and implementing media. Also, by controlling promotion and marketing they could deliver better results by establishing their multi-artist's rosters. Prior to this, the independent distributors took up most of those responsibilities. This meant each major distributor now had to provide all the services exclusively for their artists and product. As a result, there was high demand for seasoned record promoters, press, and marketing people formerly employed at the independent distributors.

Pittsburgh, like many of the other top 20 markets, was part of this exciting music scene revolution during that era. Every market had its trend-setting radio stations who broke new talent. Radio stations were a catalyst in launching the careers of new artists. Pittsburgh had stations like KQV, KDKA, WAMO, WIXZ, WTAE, and WZUM all with playlists of 40 to 60 records. The Program Directors, (PDs), and Music Directors, (MDs), were people willing to take a chance by playing new records and new artists. Disc Jockeys would talk about new artists and the music they were playing. When Chuck Brinkman at KQV, Porky Chedwick at WAMO, Bob Mac and Mad Mike at WZUM or Terry Lee at WMCK added a new record to their radio show, it only took a couple days for request lines to light up and retail stores to start getting calls.

This was an amazing time to break a new artist. The record labels knew that a great response in one market would make it easier to spread success to other markets with similar demographics. The music industry at the time provided many great employment opportunities, records and tapes were selling in big numbers, and the major labels wasted no time in cherry picking the employees from their former distributors.

When I graduated high school, I was accepted at California State Teachers College in rural Pennsylvania. While taking 17 credits per semester, I would commute from home on Mondays, Wednesdays, and Fridays. On alternating Saturdays, I worked either at Chuck's Record Shop or my uncle's Gulf Gas Station across from the Betis Atomic Plant, changing oil and washing cars. Tuesdays and Thursdays were reserved for my unpaid role as the oldies record specialist and promotions assistant at Fenway Record Distributor in Pittsburgh. At Chuck's, I earned $2.00 an hour and could buy new product at his wholesale cost. The gas station paid $1.75 an hour for pumping gas, running for parts and hand washing cars. Although my role at Fenway was initially unpaid, it gave me invaluable experience in the music business. My boss, Nick Cenci, allowed me to keep as many promotional records as I wanted. Those records, stamped as "Promo" or "DJ Copy," were crucial for generating interest in new music delivered to radio and retail. Sorting and distributing those records gave me direct access to emerging artists and new trends. As my collection grew, I felt like I had hit the jackpot between the discount records from Chuck, and free records from Fenway.

Fenway was owned by Herb Cohen and Nick Cenci, both seasoned professionals in the music business. Around the holidays, Herb would hand out bonus checks to everyone, even to me, the unpaid intern. He then would offer to cash the checks and invite everyone to a craps game in the warehouse. I owe a lot to the Fenway experience. The exposure to key record executives, radio and TV personalities, and retail outlets, set the stage for an interesting music business career.

During my sophomore year of college, an opportunity arose to work as a full-time promotion man at Hamburg Brothers, another major independent distributor in Pittsburgh. At the time, Fenway and Hamburg Brothers were the city's largest distributors, each representing over 100 record labels. Fenway was best known for distributing Motown Records, Roulette Records, numerous subsidiary labels like Rama, End, and Gone labels owned by Berry Gordy, Morris Levy, George Goldner and Joe Kolsky. Hamburg Brothers represented major labels like RCA, Atlantic, Warner Brothers, Elektra, as well as a host of smaller independent record labels.

Everyone on the floor at both Fenway and Hamburg referred to me as Cossie. When record label heads visited our distributor looking for answers regarding radio airplay, they were directed to see Cossie. Every record label representative would then ask, what's your first name? Instead of reiterating the entire name and background story...'well Cosmo was my nick name, then shortened to Cos, then Cossie, in high school, based on the Sunday funnies character from Beetle Bailey, and at the gym I boxed, etc. etc....It was far more expeditious to just say...Tom'. For the next 60 years, everyone in the record business knew me by Tom Cossie. Many years later when I lived in Burbank, I even had a California's driver's license as Tom Cossie. What's in a name. I was a Polish/German kid with an Italian sounding name surrounded by Record Business friends who were either Jewish, African American or Italians. My life was an assimilation of nationalities and cultures.

During the major record labels transition in the late 60's, new product rollout meetings took place all the time as major labels would schmooze the local distributors with parties and presentations. Atlantic, Warner Brothers, and Electra records once held one of these extravaganzas in Palm Springs. As the promotion man for Hamburg Brothers, I gladly attended. During Atlantic's presentation I met some personal record industry legends: Ahmet and Nasua Ertegun, producer extraordinaire Jerry Wexler, along with Jerry Greenberg, who was then Atlantic's VP of promotion. Those open luncheons, dinners, and the meet-and-greet time paid great dividends. I had the opportunity to talk records with the Major labels and the men who made the record industry possible. During that initial meeting with Ahmet Ertegun, I mentioned one of my favorite early Atlantic recordings was by Sticks Magee's "Drinking Wine Spo-Dee-O-Dee."

Ahmet smiled at the fact I knew the record, which was one of his first releases on Atlantic Records in 1950.

My passion for music, record collecting experience, and early interactions with label owners laid a strong foundation for my music industry career.

Ten years later, Jerry Greenberg would become President of Atlantic Records. Having worked with Jerry over the years, he knew I would bring additional promotional resources should he acquire one of my artists to his label. That was to be the case when Marc Kreiner and I signed Chic to Atlantic Records in 1977.

Chapter Four

The Mind Garage Electric Liturgy

Before my journey to NYC and working directly for RCA Records, I had a significant career milestone while still in college by signing a group called The Mind Garage to RCA in 1965. At the time, we also received a record contract offer from Atlantic Records. Both companies would go on to play pivotal roles in recording and promoting artists in the years to come. The mid- 60's may feel like ancient history, but for some of us it feels like yesterday.

Back in 1965, while working at Hamburg Brothers, I produced and managed The Mind Garage. They had a strong local following playing at clubs in the college town of Morgantown, West Virginia. I was just 18, in college, working for a record distributor, and managed to secure a two-album deal with RCA in New York, not bad for your first band. The Mind Garage had carved out a unique niche, creating what we called "The Electric Liturgy." The band performed this liturgy in collaboration with several prominent Episcopal churches in NYC, including St. Mark's Church in the Bowery and Trinity Church on Wall Street. The Mind Garage also had a dear friend and sponsor: Reverend Michael Payne, an Episcopal minister and grandson of the prominent Payne family, known for their ties to Payne, Jackson, Weber, and Curtis of the New York Stock Exchange. Reverend Payne's high-society connections and Episcopal Church network were instrumental in opening doors and providing the band with crucial support.

The RCA recording contract materialized after two key events. The first was The Mind Garage's performance of The Electric Liturgy at St. Mark's Church on 2nd Avenue in the Bowery. That event resulted from the Reverend Payne's invitation to perform at a family gathering at the prestigious Piping Rock Country Club in upstate New York.

Upon arrival at Piping Rock, we felt a little out of place, a group of hippies, amidst the well-heeled. Reverend Payne gave us a quick tour, showing us the stage area for the sound check. During the tour, I noticed a set of antique golf clubs mounted on the wall, which I later learned had belonged to President Taft. Piping Rock dated back to the early 1900's and boasted a membership that included business tycoons like the Vanderbilts, Dick Astor, and J.P. Morgan. The juxtaposition of our psychedelic band performing there felt like an oxymoron: hippies meet high society.

That evening's performance turned into a cultural exchange and a resounding success. The Payne family and their debutante ball guests were thrilled, and so was the band. We earned $3,000 for a one-hour set—six times what we'd usually earn for a full three set evening in West Virginia. This generous payment covered most of our travel and living expenses for the week in New York, including a four-hour recording session at Bell Sound Studios and performances of The Electric Liturgy at St. Mark's and Trinity Church. Out of gratitude for Reverend Payne's hospitality, we agreed to play the church events without compensation. The Manhattan performances permitted the band to invite representatives from RCA, Atlantic, and other record companies to see The Mind Garage in action.

BR- Ted Smith, Jack Bonasso, FR- Norris Lytton,
Larry McClurg, John Von.
Photo by Bob Campioni

You might wonder how a rock band performing the Electric Liturgy ended up playing at a debutante ball and two Episcopal churches. The answer lies in their repertoire. The Mind Garage's set list blended original compositions with arrangements of contemporary popular songs. These songs conveyed messages of love and peace, values cherished by all religions and emblematic of the 1960's cultural climate.

Two standout cover songs were *"Reach Out, I'll Be There"* by The Four Tops and *"Get Together"* by The Youngbloods. Both songs carried profound lyrical messages:

The Four Tops - "Reach Out, I'll Be There" (1966)

Now if you feel that you can't go on

Because all of your hope is gone

And your life is filled with much confusion

Until happiness is just an illusion

And your world around is crumbling down...

The Youngbloods - "Get Together" (1965)

Come on, people now

Smile on your brother

Everybody get together

Try to love one another right now.

The Mind Garage's focus on love, peace, and joy resonated deeply during the psychedelic era. The Sunday performance at St. Mark's Church was scheduled for 11:00 a.m., and the band rehearsed for three days at Reverend Allan's Episcopal Church. The stage was meticulously planned: the altar served as the focal point; with drummer Ted Smith, and bassist Norris Lyton positioned behind it. Lead vocalist Larry McClurg, Jack Bonasso, and guitarist John Vaughn stood center stage between the celebrants and rhythm section. This setup, combined with Reverend Allan's participation, made for a truly integrated Mass for this Electric Liturgy. The Youngbloods' *"Get Together"* became part of the Communion hymnal, while The Four Tops' *"Reach Out, I'll Be There"* was incorporated into the Gospel reading. It was a spiritually uplifting service that drew an unusually large crowd for an otherwise traditional 11:00 a.m. service. That memorable Sunday included representatives from RCA and Atlantic, as well as Pete Traynor, the developer of Traynor sound equipment.

The Reverend Michael Allen, Pastor at St, Marks, told the band and I that when they passed the collection baskets at mass, the band would receive all the proceeds as an extra thank you for the performance. I'll never forget emptying out the baskets having the aroma of cannabis mingled in with dollars and coins. There was a substantial amount of rolled joints and packets of choice herb included in the offering. Now every Sunday when

I go to mass at St. John The XXIII in Ft. Myers, Florida, when the collection basket comes by, my mind reverts back to those days at St. Marks in the Bowery.

(Photo by Allen Appell)

One of the major factors in securing the RCA deal was the demo recording. With funds from the Piping Rock performance, I booked a session at Bell Sound Studios. Although considered state-of-the-art at the time, the studio only had a three-track tape recorder. This meant instruments had to be grouped onto tracks: drums and bass on one, guitars and keyboards on another, and vocals on the third. Achieving the right balance was a challenge, as any mistake required re-recording an entire track.

Robert Moog
(Photo by Jack Robinson/Hulton Archive/Getty Images)

During a break, we stumbled upon a smaller studio where an intriguing man was experimenting with a wall of patch cords and knobs. He introduced himself as Robert and explained he was perfecting "the future of music." It turned out to be Robert Moog, inventor of the Moog Synthesizer. Our keyboardist, Jack Bonasso, was at once captivated, declaring, "Cossie, I need one of those!" without fully understanding what one of those was. We released two albums on RCA before the band broke up. While The Electric Liturgy concept was innovative, it wasn't commercially viable for mainstream radio. The Band moved on, and I lost contact with its members. Years later, I saw Ted Smith at a concert, he had become The Spinners' touring drummer.

By 1968, I was 21 years old, married, and still working at Hamburg Brothers. The music industry was undergoing a seismic shift from independent to direct distribution. At a memorable Atlantic Records convention in Palm Springs, I witnessed the unveiling of a new group, Led Zeppelin. The convention also highlighted the merger of Warner Brothers, Elektra, and Atlantic into WEA, marking the start of a new era. As mentioned, major labels began cutting out independent distributors, opting for direct distribution to outlets. This transition created high demand for seasoned promoters and marketers, offering me an opportunity to further establish myself in the industry.

The Pittsburgh music scene, like many top markets, thrived during this transformative era. My experience representing multiple labels positioned me well for exciting new chapters of life in the music business.

Chapter Five

RCA Family 1967 to 1975

Hamburg Brothers, like all independent distributors, were notorious for their low pay and lack of benefits. At the age of 20, I was married, earning $125 a week, with an additional $35 weekly car and expense allowance. To make ends meet, I relied on selling hard-to-find collectors' 45's and playing records at various dance clubs. I also benefited from what the record industry called a "spiff", a bonus offered to promote certain records to gain an advantage over other releases. When I made my weekly rounds to radio stations, TV, and retail accounts, I carried a satchel of promotional records, often 50 different titles of the latest releases. With hundreds of new records dropping each week and only three or four making it onto radio playlists, competition was fierce. In order to motivate a promotional person to pay extra attention and to prioritize one record over a competitor, a financial enticement called a Spiff, a $200 to $300 bonus would be offered. A spiff was given usually to help break a new artist, and because playlists were so limited even well-known artist's records, with a proven track record, were sometimes involved in this bonus plan.

RCA Records was one of those major record companies to make the jump to direct distribution. My interview with RCA stays etched in my memory. I just happened to be in New York City on a student-teachers' field trip. It was a trip on a chartered bus with twenty other students, spending two days sightseeing and attending meetings. While exploring the vibrant heart of The Big Apple, I took the opportunity to speak with two of the New York City record labels that had offered me jobs. RCA was one of the labels who had shown interest in me since I was their promotion and marketing representative with Hamburg Brothers in Pittsburgh. RCA happened to have a strong and diversified roster, with a wide range of products: Country, Pop, R&B, and the MOR (Adult Contemporary). RCA had the hits, and I must have had 15 different RCA records at any given time being played on WEEP, (Country) KQV, (Pop) WAMO (R&B), and KDKA & WTAE (MOR) playlists.

RCA knew I was in town on this teacher's junket and invited me to stop by for a visit to their headquarters. I accepted and decided to invite several of my soon-to-be teacher classmates to join me on a tour of RCA's recording studios.

As fate would have it, Henry Mancini, a former Pittsburgher, was conducting a session of brass and string players in Studio A, one of the four studios located at the RCA Headquarters. Studio A was the largest of the four and able to accommodate a full symphony orchestra. I was fascinated by the recording process, having produced the Mind Garage just three years earlier. Studio A was both acoustically and technically the most advanced facility I'd ever seen. The jump from recording The Mind Garage on three tracks in a small room, to seeing an orchestra recording live on 48 tracks was a musical epiphany. I remember asking one of the engineers, the purpose of those huge movable baffles which protruded from the top of the walls and attached to the studio ceiling. Some of those panels were hard wood, while others were coated with some sort of sound dampening fabric. As the engineer explained, Studio A was a 100-foot by 60-foot room specifically designed for live performance and all the moving panels, housed in the ceiling 30 feet above, could be electronically positioned, which would affect the sound and tone delivered from the live orchestra's instruments. The control room was space-age in comparison to what I had worked with in previous secessions. The massive control board had 48 separate channels and two 24 track Studer tape machines with two-inch recording tape so each track recorded could be isolated and tweaked to perfection, then mixed in with adjoining tracks. This combination was a producer's dream come true. I couldn't believe how fast technology had changed in a short three-year period. This control room was also extremely comfortable. Three feet in front of the large 48 track control board was seating for up to twelve people. From this vantage point you could look through three, large, soundproof, triple pane windows and see every inch of the studio. Behind the control room console were four high end chairs on wheels to accommodate the producer, two engineers, and an open chair so the artist recording could come in and listen to playback of what was just recorded. It was equally impressive watching Henry Mancini—one of RCA's major artists, writers, and arrangers—conduct an orchestra in this dream setting. My friends and I felt like we were in a recording Disneyland.

Our group was about to head back to our hotel, in preparation for our bus journey that evening back to California State Teachers College, when Larry Douglass, the head of pop promotion who arranged the tour, told me Augie Blume and Stan Montero, two of the promotion department's senior staff, wanted to meet me. Though I was still somewhat euphoric from the studio tour, I knew I had to get back for a seminar and pack my bag for the return to college. Larry told me I should make the best of the opportunity and meet the team upstairs. During my brief days in the seminary the monsignor would always say. "When in Rome, Do as the Romans". I decided to take that advice and the studio elevator, which took Larry and me up to the tenth floor. We walked down a long hallway with doors wide open on both sides. All genres of music were being played in those offices while in other offices, people were intensely engaged in t e l e phone conversations, as mail was being delivered from a cart making its way down the hall.

The first person I met on executive row set the tone for my first day at the RCA home office. As Larry and I made our way to the end of the long hallway, walking toward us was a face I recognized from pictures from my earlier record collecting days. The man had the build of a football player, a welcoming smile, and wore what looked like a sailor captains' hat. The man was none other than Harvey Fuqua. Larry casually introduced us, and I must have shaken his hand for several minutes. I responded like a teenager who just met one of their Idols for the first time. Harvey was a legend in my eyes.

I blurted out, "The Harvey Fuqua, Harvey and the Moonglows, Etta and Harvey, Chance Records, Chess Records, Tri-Fi Records, Motown Records!" I continued by saying "Mr. Fuqua, in my record collection I think I have every record you have ever recorded." An even broader smile came to his face.

He said, "Nice to meet you, you appear to be a lot younger than your years by knowing my records... where are you from?"

I said, "Pittsburgh, I'm just in town for a visit."

Harvey grinned, "Pittsburgh! I have a lot of friends in Pittsburgh. Do you know Porky Chedwick?"

I said, "Do I know Porky Chedwick?" And was about to give him my life's story with Porky, when

Larry interrupted and said, "Harvey, I'm sure you will be seeing a lot of Tom in the future. For now, we need to make the rounds, great seeing you." At which point I think I finally stopped shaking Harvey's hand. As we parted company Larry said, "I see Harvey all the time, and had no idea of his background. For a minute it seemed like you were meeting Elvis."

I told Larry, "Even Better." I thought, now, my day was complete, but that was not to be the case, this day was just beginning.

Moments later, Larry introduced me to Augie Blume and Stan Montero, RCA's National Directors of Promotion and Artist Relations. I had spoken with them both over the phone while working at the distributor. They seemed cool and looked like they sounded over the phone, relaxed and casual. As good promotion men, they didn't waste any time and played me one of their new RCA releases. I was in their office for less than 30 seconds when those two promotion men were promoting me, a promotion man.

They told me, "Check this out, we just received the advanced promo copies, it's a very pop sounding record, but we guarantee it's a smash. It's not a real group, they're called the Archies, the singer is Ron Dante, a friend of ours, tell us what you think?"

Being more of an R&B and rock music fan, I still listened attentively. Three minutes later the song was over, I decided to choose my words wisely. I knew from experience, openly not liking another promotion man's record, would be comparable to telling a young mother that her child was ugly. My comment was, "Wow, you are right, this is one of the most pop soundings records I've ever heard. Pop, but catchy, '*Sugar, Sugar, Honey, Honey, you are my candy girl,*' cool pop lyric." Augie and Stan were right and a month later it was on every pop radio station in the country. They gave me five advanced copies to take with me. I didn't find that odd since I worked for the distributor in Pittsburgh and probably, upon my return, would find a box of those copies at my office. It seemed apparent based upon our remaining conversations; they had plans concerning my future employment with RCA.

Next stop was the 8th Floor. Or as Larry called it, Suit City. This executive floor at 1133 Avenue of the Americas, resembled scenes from *Mad Men;* skirts and suits everywhere. I even met a hot redhead who dressed and acted like the Christina Hendricks character from that Mad Man TV series. As we moved on, I met Herb Hellman, the Senior VP of Press and Media. Herb was an impeccably groomed gentleman, clad in a sharp three-piece suit, sitting behind a large desk in a beautiful upscale office. After a cordial hello, Herb escorted me into a somewhat smaller office, the walls adorned with a kaleidoscope of posters, cherished memorabilia, autographed backstage passes, photographs, and album covers. Album covers of Jefferson Airplane, Elvis, The Guess Who and other newer artists, soon to be RCA covered every inch of wall space.

Herb stated, "Tom Cossie, meet Stu Ginsberg, our director of press and publicity. I think you fellows have a lot in common." Herb had a keen sense of the obvious, recognizing the generational similarities regarding hair length and not so formal attire. I had a good feeling the moment I met Ginsberg; I knew major events would be brewing in the years to come. Stu, who I affectionately called "Stu the Jew" started the name branding process, by referring to me as "Tommy the Gentile". I told Stu early on I attended a Jesuit Seminary and told him I thought I would have made an excellent priest. Stu's reply was "Yeah right, and me a Rabbi.' I had no idea that two years later, I would be living in NYC, working my way up the RCA ladder and embarking on numerous memorable experiences with Stu, by us working together and blending press with radio promotion.

My studio tour and meetings with the executive row turned into a four-hour interview which culminated in a job offer from RCA. My final stop at headquarters that day was a meeting with the head of finance to finalize the deal. A man of stoic demeanor, aptly named Harry K.

Harry K was a bean counter in the truest sense of the word. Harry, a much older gentleman, begrudgingly started the conversation by sharing with me RCA's prepared offer: "You will work out of your home in Pittsburgh as a regional promotion man, your starting salary will be $14,800 a year, plus bonuses, a car of my choice, and an expense account."

I worked hard to contain my jubilation since this base salary was three times what I would make as a teacher, and my current expense account at Hamburg Brothers Distributor was $35 dollars a week with no car or allowance. I then asked Mr. K what my expense budget would be. He said, with a not so enthusiastic tone, "I was told to tell you, whatever it takes to get the job done, within reason." And he again repeated, "within reason." One would think Harry was placing the Hope Diamond in the hands of some young hippy kid. At least, he left me with that impression. For some reason, I felt I would be crossing paths with Mr. K in the future, sparing over contested expense account charges.

This moment would mark a pivotal crossroad in my life. Time to make a life altering decision, should I become a special education teacher next semester, and make $5,200.00 a year, or accept RCA's offer and follow a business career in the music industry at triple the salary.

That evening, the bus was to head back to California, PA. Meanwhile, RCA wanted me to start the next day. Larry Douglass told me he reserved a room for me, just a half block away at the Royalton Hotel on 44th Street. He said RCA wanted a commitment by the next morning. I remember checking into the hotel, ordering room service and making two phone calls. One call was to a student teacher friend, saying I wouldn't be taking the bus ride back to college. The other call was to my wife, Gloria. I gave her a brief update of the day, meeting Harvy Fuqua, and seeing Henry Mancini. I then told her about the RCA offer, and when I got to the part about the salary and car of my choice, there was a long moment of silence, then a loud, yet gleeful tone of voice... "Are you kidding, Take the Job, you need to ask? Take The Job."

I took the job, went shopping the next day for some additional clothes and spent the week at the home office having meetings with the National promotion team. During the first year as a full time RCA employee, I worked out of my home but was on the road most of the time getting acquainted with my new territory, which in addition to Pittsburgh included: Cleveland, Buffalo, Philadelphia and all surrounding secondary markets in between. This would be the beginning of a great adventure.

As the corporate pendulum swings, the RCA national promotion personnel moved on and the new Vice president of Promotion, Frank Mancini, was brought in to run the operation. It was 1970 and with his new appointment as department head, Frank asked me to move to NYC to become the new National Album Promotion Director.

Simultaneously he asked another Pittsburgh native, Frank Dileo, to be his National Singles

Promotion Director.

Frank or "Tookie" as we called him, was working for Columbia records out of Cleveland, and we would both report directly to Frank Mancini.

In my years at RCA Records, I worked with a cast of friends in the press, promotion, sales, and marketing departments. Our mission was to develop artists' careers and have as much fun as possible in the process.

RCA's promotion team was one of the best in the business delivering hit singles (vinyl 45 rpm records), as well as hit albums (vinyl 33 rpm records), on the Billboard, Cash Box and Record World charts. Our RCA promotion, press and marketing team was the catalyst for developing a roster of over 150 recording artists in the late 1960's though the mid-1970's consisting of Country, Pop, Rock, R&B, and Classical music.

Chapter Six

Trade Magazines and Tip Sheets Billboard–Cash Box–Record World

One of the key promotional outlets for record reviews, placing stories, and seeing the results through chart numbers were the trade magazines and tip sheets. The big three competitive weekly trade magazines in the 60's through the 90's were Billboard, Cash Box and Record World. All three had offices in NYC and Los Angeles. Our national promotion team would service both coasts with the latest releases. Our trade magazine specialists; Karen "Nancy Drew" Williams in New York City, and Georgeann Galante in Los Angeles would make sure the trades were updated with statistics on each of our priority releases. Each trade would print their list of the nation's most popular 100 singles as well as top 200 Albums. All three reported on every music category with charts representing success on Top 40 or Pop Charts, Country Charts, R&B Charts, Easy Listening Charts, Classical Charts, Jazz Charts, and Christian Music Charts. There was a chart for every current form of music released.

There was a process to obtain chart status for both singles and albums. The singles charts were compiled based on radio station chart numbers and airplay. The trades would evaluate each record, which ones were added or dropped, and track the movement of each record position up or down local radio station charts. They would track hundreds of radio stations across the country and categorize each station with their own weight rating system. For example, the number one station in a major market like Chicago, WLS or WGCL, would receive 5 points, where in a smaller market, the number one stations would carry a point rating between 1 and 4 on a weight scale. All records nationally would then be funneled into a system to determine what records were hot and the ones that were not. Sounds complicated, however it turned out to be a relatively accurate way to determine where a song would land on a national chart.

Literally hundreds of radio stations were tracked each week. Movement on those stations' local charts, would determine the movement of the industry trade charts. Billboard, Cash Box and Record World were often in sync with each other with only slight variations in their numerical rankings. Each trade would have their own panel of key radio stations broken down by each separate music category. The album charts were compiled based strictly upon record sales. Distribution was key to achieving positive album chart status.

With similarity to radio stations, key retail outlets were also contacted by record labels on a weekly basis to make sure the product was placed properly and sales re-orders were reported. The role of promotion and sales representatives was to remind outlets to report their product's sales performance when trades called in order to influence chart placement. Regardless of merit, a positive report was always encouraged. The comparison between sales outlets and radio stations ends there.

Unlike radio stations, independent stores, one-stop wholesale accounts, and retail chain outlets were not subject to the FCC rules and regulations regarding payola or other forms of inducements. Retail sales outlets were prime targets for creative marketing. Because competition was brisk, extra products, called free goods, would be given to stores to insure a more favorable report to the trades. Competition became intense as record labels competed for top 10 chart status. The term "Free Goods" was often built into recording contracts so record labels did not have to pay the artist royalties on records given away to help influence chart movement.

In the summer of 1974, while I was serving as Vice President of promotion at RCA, our team had three records in the top five across the Billboard, Cash Box, and Record World charts. The records included: 'Rock the Boat' by The Hughs Corporation, 'Everybody Plays the Fool' by

The Main Ingredient, and '*Daddy, Don't You Walk So Fast*' by Wayne Newton. The objective was to secure the first, second, and third positions on the charts. A milestone which had never been achieved. T.K. Records, under the promotion and marketing leadership of a dear friend, Young Howard Smiley, kept RCA from achieving that unique goal with the hit single, '*Rock Your Baby*', by George McCrae, which occupied number one of those top five positions. I suppose if you are going to be denied a unique achievement it is best served by a good friend.

The mid 70's was a successful time for our artists on the RCA Label. One month we had 18 records on the country's top 100 charts, 15 singles on the top 100 pop charts, and 20 albums on the top 200 album charts. While our promotion, marketing, and sales team deserve credit, it was uncommon for a company to achieve such success in a short period. I believe the timing of key releases and the quality of our product played the most significant role. I also had the best promotion team in the business.

The Tip Sheets

Tip Sheets were a record industry staple, and a key vehicle in promoting and exposing a new artist to radio stations both regionally and nationally. Weekly Tip Sheets like Radio and Records, and the Bob Hamilton Report, were based out of Los Angeles, The Friday Morning Quarterback was headquartered in Cherry Hill NJ, Mickey Turntable, in Buffalo, The Gavin Report was in San Francisco and The Bobby Poe Report was based out of Washington DC. While the big three trades were 4 color glossy printed magazines, the Tip Sheets varied in look and design. Some were in magazine format and others were stapled sheets of letter or legal sized paper. Like the big three trades they all, except for The Gavin Report, accepted advertising. Those tip sheets were especially important to smaller market radio stations. Tip Sheets gave those stations a voice and identification in the national marketplace. The smaller market radio stations played a major role in building interest in new artists. Proven artists who had a successful music track record would receive early airplay in major markets based upon artist familiarity. New artists didn't have that luxury. Record labels would build grassroots campaigns through the Tip Sheets. Without the Tip Sheets most of the secondary stations, and no third level small market stations, would have had national visibility. Most of those radio stations did not receive free promotion records before reporting to the Tip Sheets. They played what they thought exceptional and relevant to their audience. In short order, small market radio station's program directors and music directors became important players thanks to the visibility given to them through Tip Sheets.

Chapter Seven

Michael Nesmith And

Trip to Whistler Mountain

As a regional field representative for RCA, and prior to moving to New York City, I would attend as many trade and tip sheet conventions as possible. Those events would give all the radio station programmers and record company promotion people time to participate in workshop panels and socialize while having a few drinks. One such record radio junket took place at a lodge on Whistler Mountain in Canada, about a two-hour drive north of Vancouver. It was the winter of 1969, and this event was hosted by the Bob Hamilton Report. Recently I decided to look up the current guest accommodations at Whistler Mountain, believe me, that Ski destination now looks nothing like it did back then. It's amazing how our desire for creature comforts has evolved.

The Whistler Mountain's Ski Lodge base camp was this events destination. The meeting schedules were sent out in advance. The meetings and artist performances would take place at the top of the mountain, accessible by traveling halfway up in a six-passenger gondola, then jumping on an open-air T-bar ski lift that carried you up past the tree line and into the camp summit. The lift part of the trip was both frigid chilling and exciting chilling. I don't think 55 years ago safety was a major concern. A lot of the older people opted not to take the T-bar to the top for the main event meetings; therefore, some events took place at the lodge and bar area located at the halfway point.

These convention events were oftentimes located at unique locations, with top celebrities in attendance. This gathering hosted three of RCA's artists; Michael Nesmith, John Denver, BW Stevenson whose new record, 'My Maria', was just released, Cheech and Chong were there promoting a new film, and book author Doctor Harris gave a reading of his new book, "I'm OK, You're Ok". Record industry conventions and gatherings like these presented a key opportunity to expose a new artist or have an established artist either perform or just mingle and get to know all the radio station program directors, music directors and record company executives.

Our journey to this event began at the airport in Vancouver, BC. RCA's legendary promotion duo, Augie Blume and Stan Montero, rented a large Winnebago, and invited Larry Douglass, my wife Gloria, me and Michael Nesmith to join them on our drive north to Whistler. Michael, aside from being the leader of his former group, The Monkeys, had three albums on RCA in the late 60's. He was a kind soul, great musician, and once you met him, you knew quickly he was going to be a friend. It wasn't until much later I found out Michael's mom, was the inventor of *Whiteout*, that miracle white stuff that corrected bad typing errors during the days of the typewriter.

Jerry Morris, RCA's Seattle promotion man. was the designated driver. The drive should have taken two hours but once we got underway a weather front moved in. We were heading up Rt. 99 through mountain passes. The music was rocking, Jerry had a doobie hanging from his lips, and the party to Whistler was underway. It was late in the evening as we were winding up the fog laden mountain roads. I was sitting at a round table in the back of the van, listening to music, smoking some of Augie's herb, and drinking. I thought I'd see how our driver was doing after making a few quick turns and seemingly riding over some rough terrain. I walked up to the front of the van, looked out through the windshield and not seeing the road told Jerry to immediately stop the Van. When you smoke a little weed sometimes your eyes can play tricks on you. Tricks or no tricks, I could not see the road. Jerry came to a dead stop.

Jerry and I walked out the side van door onto a rough gravel area. The van's headlights were shining into a vast curtain of impenetrable fog. I had no idea how he was able to drive. I found a large rock on the ground and threw it as far as I could in the direction we were headed; there was no sound of the rock striking anything; not tree, not other rocks, not ground. Nothing. Jerry went back in and asked Michael, Larry and Stan to check this out. We slowly inched our way forward and paused about ten feet away from the van and stood directly in front of it. I threw one more stone into the abyss only to hear, five seconds later, a splash in the water. Jerry, Larry, Michael, Stan, and I took a few more hits off Augie's remarkable private stash and got back in the van. Jerry slowly backed up the Van onto the paved road then very slowly headed off into the night. I guess this was not our time to leave this planet. Having traveled to many locations with notable recording artists I often thought, when traveling with a high-profile artist, if the plane went down, or a deadly accident occurred involving myself and a star, I probably wouldn't get a mention in the obituary. Sad thought but true.

When I heard about Michael's passing away this past year, I asked my wife Gloria, who was with us that memorable evening, if she remembered that journey to Whistler's Mountain with Michael Nesmith. She said, "I sure do, I was the only one not high on Augie herb and it was amazing you guys even noticed the fog outside since there was probably an equal amount of foggy smoke inside the Van".

Fortunately for us, we made it to Whistler, and all passengers arrived safe and relatively sound.

Chapter Eight

The Industrial Diamond Caper

Stu *the Jew* and Tommy *the Gentile's* Big Adventure

It was a cool late spring Sunday morning in 1973. Stu Ginsburg (Stu the Jew of this story) and I, along with Harry Nilsson and Derek Taylor, were flying from NYC to Boston. Our mission? A six-city major market press and radio tour, starting in Boston, to launch a special new album, titled *A Little Touch of Schmilsson in the Night*. This album of 15 classic standards, including songs like *'Lazy Moon', 'It Had to Be You',* and *'As Time Goes By',* marked a departure from Harry's previous albums. I remember Harry sharing his excitement, saying he was glad to record these timeless classics while he still had the voice of a Sinatra-style crooner. Harry cherished recording in London, fueled by his close friendship with The Beatles and Derek Taylor—a British journalist, writer, publicist, and record producer. Derek, often called the "Fifth Beatle," shared the title with Harry at times as well as George Martin, the Beatles producer.

I was a fan of Harry Nilsson long before we met. Before my time at RCA, Harry had recorded two of my favorite albums: *Pandemonium Shadow Show* and *Aerial Ballet*. A prolific writer, Harry penned most of the songs on *Aerial Ballet*, including *'One (One is the loneliest number)'*. Years later, a more up-tempo version of *One*, became a Top 10 hit for Three Dog Night. *'Everybody's Talkin'* was another standout track from the album, written by Fred Neil.

Pandemonium Shadow Show, another masterpiece, was the work which introduced Harry to The Beatles. Derek loved the album so much that he sent copies to each of the Beatles. Harry wrote six of the 12 songs on that album, which also included two Beatles covers along with *'1941'*, Derek's favorite song. The Beatles appreciated Harry's talent and embraced him into their inner circle. A few years later, both Ringo Starr and John Lennon collaborated with Harry on various record and film projects. Ringo and Harry starred in a movie called Son of Dracula. Harry played Count Down and Ringo was Merlin the Magician. Around the same time John Lennon and Harry collectively worked on an album containing the song, 'Many Rivers to Cross'. A project which turned out to be, in my opinion, a vocal low point in an amazing artist's career. A more in-depth story to follow.

We were riding high off the success of *Nilsson Schmilsson*, Harry's most commercially successful album to date, released by RCA in November 1971. It featured three of his most iconic songs: the No. 1 hit '*Without You*' (originally recorded by Badfinger), '*Jump into the Fire*', and '*Coconut*'. Harry recorded the album in his beloved London and worked with legendary producer Richard Perry. In 1973, Harry's rendition of '*Without You*' won the Grammy Award for Best Male Pop Vocal Performance.

Perhaps you were wondering, what do industrial diamonds have to do with this story? Well, the clues include Boston's John Hancock Building, four hungover sailors (or rather, music businesspeople), two bottles of Crown Royal, a bottle of Bell's Scotch, and a layer of chromium, sandwiched between sections of ridged glass. It all began in NYC.

Harry, Derek, Stu, and I attended an event at the Plaza Hotel's Oyster Bar. That evening, Stu and I enjoyed listening to Harry and Derek reminisce about British musicians and many recording sessions at Trident Studios, one of the most popular recording locations in London. I didn't know Derek before he produced Harry's newest album, but I quickly learned about his illustrious career and musical background. The bar closed at 3:00 a.m., and we had an 8:10 a.m. flight to Boston. Before leaving, Derek ordered four shots of Fernet Branca and said, "Drink this; it'll sober you up in seconds." Surprisingly, it worked—and we made our flight.

Don "Captain Spacy" Delacy, our star New England RCA promotion manager, greeted us at the Boston arrival gate. Back then, you could meet people at the gate. Don was waiting with a copy of the Boston Globe Sunday Edition. He also informed us he had three bottles of our favorite beverages waiting at the hotel. Don, a music aficionado and favorite among Boston radio station DJ's and Music Directors, had an impressive background. One Boston journalist, and author of Counterculture in Boston, described him as "the laid-back master of iconic understatement." Before joining RCA, Don was a captain of one of Boston's star attractions, the Swan Boat, which would navigate the pond on Boston Commons. The Swan Boat was the social catalyst where he built many media connections.

We stayed at The Colonnade, a beautiful, centrally located hotel, perfect for conducting interviews with the press, TV, and radio program directors. Harry was at the peak of his recording career, however, never did live performances, and rarely did interviews. This forthcoming six-city tour was highly anticipated based upon his popularity and rarity of appearances. As a result, every hour of our schedule, from 8 a.m. to 5 p.m., was packed with media appointments.

That Sunday morning, in route to the hotel, Harry read aloud a Boston Globe front-page headline about windows blowing out of the John Hancock Building. He said, "We need to visit this site once we check in". Don took us to our rooms, dropped off our bags, and had a quick, much needed, "hair of the dog". Don, being a man of detail, had a full bar set up in Harry's suite. Once situated we embarked on our walking tour to the Hancock Building. Derek, still recovering from the Plaza Hotel and the former nights activities, opted out of this mission.

Don led us past several streets roped off with yellow caution tape. As Stu, Don, and I speculated about what possibly could have happened regarding the demise of this skyscraper and the sparkling streets surrounding the building, we noticed Harry on the other side of the caution tape chatting with an elderly maintenance worker who was sweeping up thousands of dime-sized crystals of fractured glass, glittering in the sunlight. The streets were eerily deserted. It was Sunday morning in Catholic Boston, we guessed most people were likely at church.

To Harry's unheard question, the maintenance worker explained, "I told them! I've worked these streets for years, back when this was part of the bay. This whole area is landfill, and that building is sinking. That's why the windows are popping out."

As the worker swept the shimmering debris, Harry bent down, scooped up a handful, and exclaimed, "Industrial Diamonds! These look like industrial diamonds!"

Whether or not Harry had ever seen an actual industrial diamond, was anyone's guess, but the previous night's buzz had us all in a relaxed but jovial mood. We sent Don back to the hotel to grab two purple velvet Crown Royal sacks. When he returned, we stuffed both sacks full of those glittering dime shaped chips of glass. I gave the worker a twenty-dollar bill and thanked him for his discretion. We felt like we had just pulled off a major heist, absconding with two bags of precious rocks.

As we walked away, I heard our confidence man, favorite materials manager, and street sweeper say, 'Crazy white boys.'

Harry Displaying the Goods

That evening we dined at an elegant restaurant, The Half Shell, where we reviewed the day's successful diamond caper. and discussed Monday's itinerary. The meetings with Harry were scheduled to take place in his luxury suite, which featured a spacious living room complete with two chairs, a plush couch, a special full bar area, and a large glass coffee table as the room's centerpiece. On the table, we strategically placed copies of the new album, *A Little Touch of Schmilsson in the Night*, as samples for our attending media guests. For reasons that remain a mystery, one of the Crown Royal bags was left on the table—slightly open, its contents trailing out of the Crown Royal sack and onto the glass table.

Midway through the first interview with WBCN, Boston's premier FM rock station, the program director noticed the bag and said, "Hey Harry, something shiny is falling out of that Crown Royal bag." Without missing a beat, Harry, sitting across the room, sauntered over to the coffee table, dramatically reached down and let several more 'Industrial Diamonds' spill onto the glass surface. With the confidence of a seasoned performer, Harry quipped, "I was on vacation in South Africa, and a friend of mine handed me a brown paper bag loaded with these industrial diamonds and told me not to tell anyone where I got them or who gave them to me." He grinned, "Don, would you mind grabbing some tissues? I think our friends here deserve a little memento of my visit besides the new album." Harry ceremoniously wrapped each diamond in a tissue and handed one to every member of the WBCN crew. They all appeared enthralled, now convinced this was the coolest gift they'd ever received. Probably, until they left and had a closer look. Then again, this was the same group of people who had taken a trip on one of Captain Don's famous Swan Boat rides.

The next stop on our media tour was Chicago. With an ample supply of industrial diamonds still in our possession, we replicated the Boston event with precision. At the Downtown Regency Hotel, the velvet Crown Royal bag was once again placed conspicuously on the coffee table, alongside Harry's new album. Chicago's media crowd, much like Boston's, was captivated by Harry's tales of his South African treasures.

That evening, Harry expressed a desire to find an unassuming bar beneath the Chicago L. We received an excellent recommendation which led us to a seedy dive bar that lived up to Harry's expectations. After several rounds of drinks, Stu and I noticed that Harry had brought along one of the velvet bags. As the evening wore on, Harry dramatically pulled the bag from his jacket, placed it beside his scotch, and regaled the remaining patrons with stories of his South African adventure.

"They call them industrial diamonds for a reason," he proclaimed, holding one up to the dim light of the back bar. I nodded, gesturing it was all true.

As the night grew late, the crowd thinned to just the three of us, the bartender, and a few locals at the bar. Stu stepped outside to call a cab, and I excused myself to the restroom.

A few moments later, Harry came into the men's room and said, "I left the bag of diamonds on the bar, I wanted to see what would happen." Moments later, we walked out to discover the bar was eerily empty.

The bartender reappeared, looking as bewildered as we were. "Holy hell," he exclaimed, "where'd everybody go?"

The velvet bag, of course, was gone. Stu came running back into the bar thinking there was a fire or some other crisis taking place. He said "I saw three guys bolting out of the front entrance and running full speed down the block. What Happened?"

Harry calmly said. "We are now out of 'Industrial Diamonds.'

On the third day of the tour, we arrived in Miami and checked into the famous landmark hotel, The Fontainebleau. Harry loved this hotel, not only for its saltwater swimming pool, but also for its history as a favorite haunt of the Rat Pack: Dean Martin, Frank Sinatra, Peter Lawford, and Sammy Davis Jr.

With two free days before our next round of interviews, we lounged poolside, Stu and Harry were sadly reminiscing about our lack of diamonds. Harry, with a sad tone of voice said, "Guys, it will be rough moving forward without a supply of 'Industrial Diamonds', but the show must go on."

I am embarrassed to say, sitting by the pool with Stu and Harry was probably the first time in four days that the three of us were all sober. I remember thinking, 'Why on earth would we create this Industrial Diamonds Caper. There had to be some mind-altering forces compelling us to come up with this ruse.' Derek had seen the writing on the wall that first morning in Boston and decided to head back to England.

I then reassured Harry and Stu, "Not to worry, before we left Chicago, I called Don and asked him to make another trip to our diamond mine in Boston, aka, The John Hancock building."

The following morning, we were relaxing again by the pool when a hotel attendant approached and asked if I was Tom Cossie. I said yes, and for a moment, thought there might be an issue with our bill or reservation. He politely said, "Mr. Cossie, could you please come with me." I followed him back into the hotel lobby. He promptly introduced me to the hotel manager who said, "Mr. Cossie, We have the package I'm sure you have been waiting for." For the moment, I was a bit confused. The hotel manager then walked me to a secure area behind the front desk and into a large office. He opened a safe and handed me a tightly wrapped package addressed to me, as a guest of the hotel. Boldly written across the top of the overnight package were the words: "CONTAINS INDUSTRIAL DIAMONDS."

Rumor had it Don met some trouble on his second "diamond run." He was stopped by the police, though managed to charm his way out of an arrest by claiming to the police that the broken glass was industrial diamonds and he was just gathering samples for shipment. Based upon our diamond delivery in Florida, Don had obviously walked away with his pockets full of diamonds.

I think one of three things could have happened during those two nights earlier. One, the police were called away or directed to a more serious crime. Two, the police just let him keep the broken glass, telling him never to cross a caution tape again while dreading the idea of filling out a police report involving imaginary industrial diamonds. Three, those friendly officers, while off duty, must have in the past, taken a ride on one of Captain Don's famous Swan Boat rides.

Chapter Nine

Ziggy - It's All Hunky Dory

In the late 60's and early 70's, while I was living in New York City and working at RCA, attorney Dennis Katz, a former CBS attorney, joined RCA as the head of A&R. He signed both David Bowie and Lou Reed to RCA, two monumental steps in reshaping the music landscape. Dennis, alongside a dedicated team that included Stu Ginsburg, Frank "Tookie" Dileo, and my staff, played pivotal roles in developing and launching Bowie's career.

In 1970, I held the position of Director of National Album Promotion at RCA, Tookie managed Singles Promotion, and Ginsburg was the Director of Press. It was during this time that Dennis and Bob Ring, one of his A&R directors, presented me with three new songs by Bowie in my office. Among them was "Changes," a single that would eventually mark the beginning of Bowie's celebrated journey with RCA.

Dennis asked if our promotion team could successfully launch this artist at FM rock and pop radio stations here in the USA. My first reaction was that the music was fantastic. However, unfamiliar with Bowie at the time, I questioned, "Has David Bowie ever released records before?"

Dennis replied, "I think he had a few successful albums in England on Mercury or London Records, but no action here in the states."

David Bowie was indeed a fresh name to most Americans. Little did I realize he was quite the success in the UK and had several very successful singles and a self-titled 1969 album, *David Bowie*, featuring the UK #1 hit, *Space Oddity*. Looking back, I can now see the irony, after five years of relentless effort and a catalogue of releases, Bowie would now become an "overnight success" with his first release in the United States, *Hunky Dory*.

Recording an album was no small investment for a record label. The cost ranged from $75,000 to $150,000 for production alone, with studio sessions averaging $250 per hour at premier New York City studios like Power Station, Hit Factory, and Sigma Sound. Add in equipment rentals, background singers, and the top secession players, at double or triple scale, would also add to the cost of producing a record. And that was just the beginning.

Launching a new artist required an even heftier financial commitment, including hiring independent promoters and covering marketing shortfalls—commonly referred to as tour support. Those costs often exceeded $200,000. I knew if we launched a campaign for Bowie, his former label, Mercury, would surely capitalize on RCA's promotional efforts. My case in point: as RCA's promotional push on our first Bowie single, "Changes" gained traction, Mercury could then release a track from their catalogue to ride the wave of our momentum.

Another fascinating industry trend at the time was the "cover tune" phenomenon. If an unknown artist released a great song, a major artist would record and release their version before the original artist gained significant attention. Music publishers encouraged this practice since they benefited from royalties regardless of who recorded the song. Many of the early English pop and rock artists like the Beatles and Stones took advantage of many of our soulful R&B artists with covers from the music of Chuck Berry, Little Richard and the Isley Brothers.

Before RCA committed to signing Bowie, we approached Mercury to purchase the rights of his two earlier albums. It was a bold move, considering the risk and expense involved. Bowie was largely unknown in the U.S., so acquiring these albums was a leap of faith. In hindsight, it was a brilliant decision. The two albums, *The Man Who Sold the World* and *Space Oddity*, eventually became multimillion-sellers under RCA's banner. That year, RCA released the album, *Hunky Dory*. And David became the "darling of the press," a title we supported through strategic advertising.

Despite moderate initial success on pop and FM radio, the album's sales started slowly.

However, as press coverage, radio airplay, and marketing efforts converged, both *Hunky Dory* and the single *'Changes'* slowly climbed the charts. David's unique artistic vision and comfort with transformation made *'Changes'* a fitting debut single. David was obviously a gifted writer and poet.

The lyrics in Changes are profound with the repetitive line after every intriguing verse saying: *'Time May Change Me – But I Can't Trace Time'.*

A year earlier Bowie also displayed his depth with the Number 1 Hit in England, *Space Oddity.* When I first listened to the lyrics to the single, I thought, 'this kid's lyrics are light years ahead of his age'. David and I are the same age, however, when meeting him he appeared to be a lot younger.

When one of the women in our office first heard the *'Space Oddity'* lyrics, as David was telling the story drifting off in space to his final destiny, saying planet earth is blue, never to return home, she said. " Bowie is such a romantic, repeating the line 'Tell my wife I love her very much, she knows'." I didn't think that line exactly conjured up images of other famous Romanticists: Shelly, Keats, and Byron. However, the line did fit the song and appealed greatly to married, record buying women everywhere.

I will always remember Bowie's first visit to my office. His striking hairstyle mirrored the iconic album cover, which I affectionately referred to as the "Greta Garbo pose."

Bowie, accompanied by his manager, Tony Defries—whom Stu had nicknamed, "Tony Deep Freeze"—came to discuss the album's performance. With approximately 40,000 units sold at that point, both Bowie and Tony seemed impressed, given his lack of prior commercial success in the U.S. More importantly, the album was generating reorders—a promising sign of hit potentiality.

After our brief meeting, Defries, who also represented Lou Reed, left to discuss Lou's contract with Dennis Katz, leaving Bowie and me to talk further. We talked about the synergy between press and radio in building an artist's career.

It was evident, even then, that Bowie had a deep understanding of the interplay between artistry and promotion, a rare quality that set him apart from other new artists. Then again, he really wasn't a new artist. His years of working on the way up to successful chart performances in England contributed to the advanced self-marketing skills which he displayed.

The Launch of Ziggy and The Spiders from Mars

Almost a year had passed since the launch of *Hunky Dory*, with album sales approaching 150,000 units. While it hadn't yet reached gold album status, which required national sales of over 500,000 units. 150,000 units was still quite substantial for a new artist. The entire RCA staff were united in excitement and dedication to developing David's career. We were breaking a truly artistic, cutting-edge, new artist with a great album on the charts. As a result, radio and press began revisiting his previous work, especially 'Space Oddity' and its iconic line, 'This is Major Tom to Ground Control.' Since RCA had just acquired his earlier albums, we didn't have to worry about competing releases from other companies. Instead, we faced the challenge of balancing multiple releases from the same artist in the market. Our primary focus now was to gear up for David's new release and the accompanying tour: *The Rise and Fall of Ziggy Stardust and The Spiders from Mars.*

I always liked the Warwick Hotel on 44th Street. Located just half a block from RCA, it was an elegant, historic hotel and a favorite for housing RCA artists and staff. I knew the hotel well as I'd lived there when RCA first hired me. Due to the hotel's amenities and décor, you would often cross paths with notable film celebrities from previous decades at the bar or sharing the elevator. On one occasion, I was holding a promotional meeting with some of our east coast team. Boston's finest, Don Delacy, and I were in the lobby waiting to catch an elevator to our meeting room. The elevator arrived, the door opened, and we stepped inside, immediately followed by a handsome elderly gentleman with a friendly smile. We both immediately recognized him, and Don blurted out...."Jutty Jutty Jutty." Cary Grant responded, "Hi boys welcome to New York." The Warwick was that kind of hotel. Off the grid to tourists and popular with actors and recording artists.

During the final stages of completing the Ziggy Album, David was booked at Warwick, and I was asked to stop by to check on the progress of the new album and see if David had drafted the final liner notes for the cover. When I entered

David's suite, his guitarist, Mick Ronson, was working on a song. Mick was sitting, strumming chords while David, half-reclined on a couch, sketched a portrait of Mick. Intrigued by this sight, I walked over to see his drawing. David casually showed me a professional-looking sketch of Mick with the titles of the forthcoming Ziggy album's songs written underneath. I complimented him on his sketching skills, and David's response surprised me: "If you like it, it's yours." His artistic generosity left an impression on me. Nevertheless, I needed those liner notes. I returned to headquarters, made a copy of his work, and gave it to our art department. I kept the original and stored it in a secret place.

As it turned out my secret storage place was so secret that even today, I can't remember the location of that secret place. Years ago, I told this story to a major music memorabilia collector who immediately told me, "I'll pay you ten thousand dollars should you ever find that piece of art."

My relationship with David was cordial but businesslike and I didn't see him that often. When I did, his manager, Tony Defries, was always nearby. Tony's mannerisms reminded me of other control-oriented managers I had encountered.

I've often thought Tony might have taken his artist managerial traits from the legendary Colonel Tom Parker. While there is no book entitled *How I Controlled the Career of Elvis*, it wouldn't have surprised me if someone had told Tony, "Never let your artist be alone with the record company." This practice seemed common among big name, control freak, managers like Colonel Tom Parker who managed Elvis and Jerry Weintraub, the manager of John Denver, as well as Tony who was a well-known figure in England and brought that valuable expertise to navigating London's music scene. His street smarts proved instrumental in planning the launch of Ziggy.

Interestingly, Harry Nilsson was an exception. He managed his own career without any traditional manager running interference between the artist and record label.

Over the years Harry did so successfully without touring and without a manager. Since managers make most of their money from the artist being on tour, there was probably a good reason why Harry was no prize to management. In today's world, an artist and manager would starve without touring and selling merchandise.

Frank Mancini was RCA's Senior Vice President of Promotion and Artist Relations, with a large corner office two doors down from mine. Frank was my boss. And though he shared the name, he bore no relation to Henry Mancini, another RCA luminary as a major composer, author, and performer. Both Mancini's were remarkable individuals, each in their own way. Frank often referred to Tookie Dileo and me as

Butch Cassidy and the Sundance Kid. To this day, I'm still unsure why.

Frank was the quintessential promotions department leader. He had a talent for delegating tasks and ensuring the national promotion team executed their plans flawlessly. To craft a strategy for launching *The Rise and Fall of Ziggy Stardust and The Spiders from Mars*, Frank, Stu, Herb Helman (Stu's boss), Tookie, and I spent hours exploring pre-release options and consulting Tony Defries. We ultimately devised a plan to bring 20 key press and media figures to England, David's home turf. This group included writers and magazine publishers who had supported our first critically acclaimed project, *Hunky Dory*.

We checked our entourage into two of London's most luxurious hotels: The Inn on the Park and The Dorchester. The plan was to showcase David and *The Spiders from Mars* in an intimate yet upscale pub in Aylesbury, a suburb on London's outskirts. This setting allowed us to control the sound and environment for this elite audience of critics. We chartered a luxury party bus, complete with refreshments, and took a scenic route through the countryside, passing stunning rose gardens along the way. Spirits were high when we arrived at the pub for the exclusive mini concert and first-time performance of *Ziggy and The Spiders from Mars.*

It turned out to be a memorable late afternoon performance at that pub in Alsbury, England. David and The Spiders delivered an electrifying show that captivated our group of correspondents. All without full production, wardrobe changes and special effects reserved for the major tour. Those press critics, notorious for being a tough crowd, were thoroughly impressed. The intimate setting showcased the music's power, and the buzz was immediate. When this album showcase was over, everyone agreed, a full-scale stage show based upon this performance would make a block buster tour.

We ensured they didn't have to wait long for the album launch and tour to hit the states. Those who attended the England launch party were later invited to the American premiere in February 1973 at Radio City Music Hall in New York City. The advanced press and radio coverage from the London event coupled with The Radio City performance's outstanding reviews, paved the way for a sold-out American tour and a platinum album. The rest is history.

The two albums RCA had purchased from Polygram and Mercury Records for $100,000 eventually sold over one million copies each, achieving platinum status and delivering a monumental return on investment. To this day, the seventies RCA team takes pride in being the catalyst for two of David's most iconic projects: *Hunky Dory* and *The Rise and Fall of Ziggy Stardust and The Spiders from Mars.*

I recall an interesting story following the release of the Ziggy album. Herb Helman informed me that NBC, RCA's parent company, wanted to produce a special report on the music business. Herb asked if I could aid their news crew by discussing how we launched the Bowie album and detailing our promotional strategies.

The NBC film crew spent an entire day taping my interview. I explained our promotion process, describing how the RCA team came together, starting with David's arrival at RCA. I detailed how the press department laid the foundation, while our field promotion and sales teams collectively marketed Bowie. I estimated we spent around $200,000 on advertising, time buys, and in-store promotions—a standard amount for breaking a new artist. I also gave a detailed history and process of promoting and marketing the project.

Weeks passed, and I began wondering why nothing had become of the interview. Stu informed me that the NBC special would air the following week. He told me he hadn't seen the piece but said it should be good because they are taking so much time putting it together. When I received the air date and time, I was excited to tell my family and friends to tune in. The program began with footage of numerous black limousines arriving at an airport. The headline read: NBC News 1973: Payola To my dismay, the segment framed the story around payola scandals, with a focus on corruption and drug use in the music industry. Out of the entire day I spent discussing and filming the Bowie promotion story, NBC used only a minute or two of the taping and mostly focused on the $200,000-dollar initial expenditure on the Ziggy Stardust promotion and tour support. From the opening and through the main body of this TV Special Report, drugs and corruption were the focus. My mother called after watching the entire program and asked, "Tommy, are you ok? Is there anything I need to be worried about?"

Her comments were a precursor of my wife asking me if she should be worried about anything after a book by Fredric Dannan came out in 1990 entitled The *Hit Men*. It was a book about the record industry and behind the scenes promotion though was far more concentrated on illegal activities in promoting hit records, hence the title *The Hit Men*. It wasn't a very flattering book, emphasizing corruption and payola in industry. Gloria's concern was she knew I had spoken with most of the people in that book on a regular basis. It was embarrassing to me that your own parent company, NBC, would be willing to make headlines at the expense of one of their own divisions.

Despite the misleading NBC portrayal of the music industry, including one of our artists, the exposure didn't seem harm David's career. If anything, the publicity reinforced his rising stardom.

The Ziggy album went on to become a landmark in music history, and Bowie's legacy continued to grow in becoming a major star.

David visiting Ed Salamon. KDKA Pittsburgh PA.
Photo Credit KDKA

Ed Salamon stated, "My hometown of Pittsburgh was a big factor in breaking Bowie when he signed with RCA. Paul Mawhinney at Record Rama had been a fan since Bowie's Mercury releases and championed him at a time when retailers still had major influence. Pittsburghers and RCA promo guys Tom Cossie and Bobby Zurick made Bowie happen."

Chapter Ten

The Colonel
Another Day in Las Vegas

In the 1950's, 60's, and 70's, Elvis Presley was one of the most popular recording artists and film stars in the world. Originally signed with Sun Records, his contract was bought by Colonel Tom Parker in 1955. Parker then signed Elvis to RCA, releasing the hit song "Jailhouse Rock." The Colonel was Elvis Presley's manager and partner for over 30 years. I say "partner" in addition to "manager" because, at various times, his percentage of income from record royalties, live performances, film deals, and merchandising ranged from 25% to 50%. Normally, a management contract would be between 15% and 20%. However, the Colonel justified his higher percentage by claiming Elvis was his only client and his extra percentage reflected the exclusivity of his service.

I first worked with Elvis's records at Hamburg Brothers distributor for two years before joining RCA full-time in 1969. In the six years I worked at RCA I only met Elvis twice, both times in Nashville while he was recording. Managers representing newer artists often worked the room with their artists in different departments to secure airplay consideration and marketing funds. The Colonel and Elvis never fell into that category. Elvis was perceived as a star back in the mid-50's and a superstar for decades after; he was kept under wraps. The Colonel was the single point of contact, and even then, his appearances at the company were few and far between. When he came to NYC for a visit, he was both tough business and equally shrewd.

Pat Kelleher, in our artist relations department, was the New York City RCA point person. Pat's main call to duty was handling the Colonel and coordinating all Elvis-related business at RCA. Pat's office was next to mine, and when the Colonel was in town, alerts went up ahead of his visit. The doors were closed. When he walked through the hallways, it was never smiles with flowers, only demands. Having never been previously exposed to the Colonel's wrath, I was happy to see him. I always told Pat that as talented as Elvis was, he wouldn't have been half as successful without the Colonel. Elvis would not have been the King of Rock & Roll without Colonel Tom Parker's touch, which as rumor had it, was more like a club than a touch.

One day I asked Pat why all Elvis's singles always had to have his four-color picture on the cover. It was few and far between that any artist had picture sleeves on their 45s. Pat explained when the Colonel negotiated Elvis's contract with RCA, he required that every single, up to and including the first 500,000 units, had to be in a picture sleeve. By contractually doing so, the Colonel earned 1.5 cents for every picture sleeve in addition to the record royalty because of that picture. A penny and a half may not sound like much, but when multiplied by the millions of singles Elvis sold over the years, it amounted to a small fortune. It also promoted Elvis's image in a ubiquitous fashion. A picture, in this case, was worth far more than a thousand words.

Sometimes, Frank "Tookie" Dileo, our National Single Director, Pat, and I would leave work via the 44th Street studio entrance and head to La Bourgine or referred to as Un Deux Trois for cocktails and games of liar's poker. During one of Elvis's four sold-out shows at Madison Square Garden, Pat narrated an incident involving Elvis and his entourage wanting to shop at Bloomingdale's, one of New York City's well-known department stores. I asked Pat, "Why is that a problem?"

Pat replied, "Are you kidding? If people saw Elvis shopping, it would cause pandemonium."

I asked, "How did you handle this artist relations issue? You can't tell Elvis he can't shop with his Memphis Mafia friends."

Pat said, "At the end of his gig last night at the Garden, I arranged for Bloomingdale's to reopen at midnight with limited staff and security. They helped Elvis pick out what he wanted, we paid the bill, and the store delivered everything to Memphis."

I laughed and said, "That's artist relations."

It was 1972 at our offices in New York City. We were in a planning meeting and Pat mentioned that Colonel Tom insisted on a particular slow-tempo song be the next single release. Tookie and our promotion team argued that *'Burning Love'* was receiving the most attention on the radio stations. They said if *'Burning Love'* was not released soon, the momentum could be lost, killing the song's hit potential. I was scheduled to fly out to the West Coast the next day. Pat asked if on my return I could make a stop in Las Vegas, visit the Colonel, and catch an Elvis show at the Hilton International. I agreed, and Pat arranged for the show tickets along with an early morning meeting with the Colonel.

I arrived at McCarran Airport on Friday afternoon. Looking out the window upon landing, I saw billboards along the outskirts of the runway advertising current and future shows as well as hotel deals. One prominent sign displayed just two words: "Elvis Now." I was scheduled to meet the Colonel at 8 a.m. the next morning. This sign gave me an idea, and I began formulating my pitch to persuade The Colonel that *'Burning Love'* should be the next release. My opening pitch would be my recommendation of using some of the open space on that billboard. Why not include a tag banner saying, "Coming Soon... The New Hit Single... *'Burning Love'*."

I was confident in my marketing skills, and I believed my idea to be brilliant.

Upon checking into the hotel, I found that Pat had arranged everything: the hotel room, a stage side table at the show, and a meeting with the Colonel at 8 a.m. to take place on the fourth floor of the Hilton International Hotel. My plan was to attend Charlie Pride's earlier performance in one of the hotel's smaller rooms, followed by the late Elvis show, do some gambling, and then prepare for Saturday morning's meeting with The Colonel.

Elvis's performance was remarkable, as always. He concluded with "The American Trilogy," and when he hit the "Glory, Glory Hallelujah" chorus, the orchestra built to a crescendo and the audience erupted in roaring applause. Did you ever hear a song or performance that gave you goose bumps on your arms? Listening to this performance was one of those moments. When the song ended, Elvis fell to his knees, a man rushed across the stage and draped a cape over his shoulders, then helped him off stage to a standing ovation. What a show. I've seen many live shows by many artists, and by far an Elvis performance in Vegas would be on top that list.

After leaving that stellar Elvis performance, I started walking over to one of the blackjack tables and spotted Rozene, Charlie Prides wife, heading in my direction. She had the look of concern in her eyes and said, "Cossie, you got to get Pride away from those craps table, He's over there".

I immediately thought, 'how would Pat, our artist relations guru, handle this situation?' I didn't want to upset Charlie's wife or anger our star country artist. I approached the craps table where he was taking a break after a winning streak, smiling with chips in hand. Charlie Pride was one of my favorite Nashville artists along with Dolly Parton, Ronnie Milsap and Waylon Jennings. All four were extremely talented, nice people, and just fun to be with. I asked Charlie if we could grab a drink and give him an update on his album and latest single, 'Kiss an Angle Good Morning'.

That single turned out to be a crossover pop hit. We used that term in the industry when a hit country record would cross over from country radio to mainstream pop radio. His album was also climbing the Billboard Pop Charts. Minutes later, Rozene joined us and now seemed more composed. Everything worked out, Charlie was done for the night, and finally I could get some rest. I excused myself to get a few hours of sleep before my big meeting with The Colonel.

Four hours of sleep is a lot when you're in Vegas. It was 7:50 a.m. when I arrived on the Fourth Floor. The Elevator door opened to reveal an elderly uniformed guard sitting at a small desk.

"Good morning, I'm Tom Cossie, and I have an appointment with Mr. Parker."

The guard replied, "The Colonel is expecting you, I'll buzz you in'."

To my right was a security fence, and the gate

door clicked open. I wondered, since the Colonel had this much security in the hotel, what would Presley's penthouse security look like? I later found out that Elvis had the entire top floor which could only be entered with a special key. The Colonel, with modest security, only occupied half the fourth floor, with a guard and fence. I entered the Colonel's suite and said, "Good morning, Colonel, Pat Kelleher sends you his regards." I felt a mix of nerves and excitement. After all, both Elvis and this manager were legendary.

After a brief exchange, I laid out my brilliant idea for 'Burning Love' as a billboard tag. The Colonel listened silently, then after a short pause, said, "Did you see the show last night?" I replied, "Yes sir I did, his performance was incredible, and he brought the house down with 'The American Trilogy.'"

The Colonel leaned back and said, "My boy, people fly into Las Vegas for three things: to see Elvis, to win money, and to get laid…in that order. If I could tell people Elvis was here in Vegas with one word, I would. But I can't. I need two words: Elvis Now… On billboards, if you can't say your message in three seconds on a billboard, it doesn't exist. Furthermore, Elvis doesn't sing 'Burning Love' on stage. That could be a great single, and if it's getting the action you're telling me release it.

"Tell Pat I said Hi and have a safe trip back."

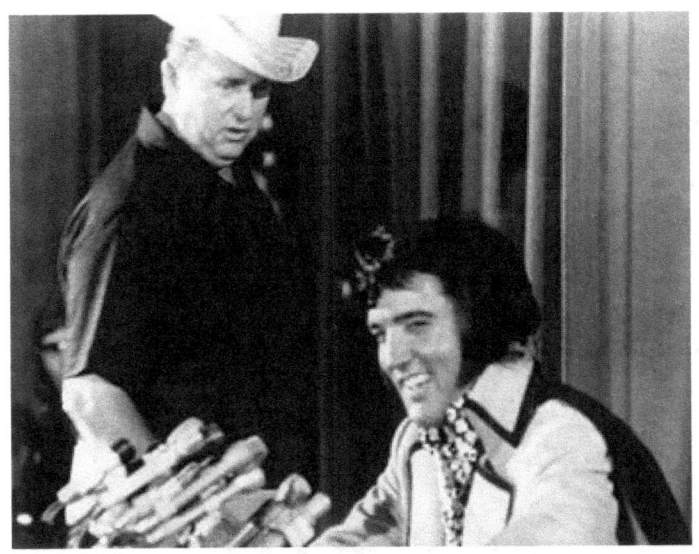

Rock and roll singer Elvis Presley holds court at a press
conference to publicize his show at Madison Square Garden
later that night while Colonel Tom Parker looks on at the Hilton
Hotel on June 9, 1972 in New York City, NY.
(Photo by Michael Ochs/Archives/Getty Images)

Quick and to the point. Mission accomplished.
As I left, I realized the Colonel's success over the
years relied on simplicity, shrewd business tactics
and no procrastination. Though he had some
tumultuous times with Elvis, I always believed
Elvis would not have become as big a star without
The Colonel's direction. As my career moved on,
I often reflected on that meeting with The Colonel.
Simplicity in advertising almost always wins the
battle. The phrase *Less is More* becomes so
relevant when it applies to framing an action,
creating an advertisement, or capturing attention.

Especially in a day and age in which people's attention span is so limited based upon the bombardment of instantaneous information.

Today, I'm proud to have a *'Burning Love'* gold record hanging in my music and wine room. When friends ask about the Colonel's portrayal in the recent Elvis film, I tell them based on my limited meetings, I thought Tom Hanks did a great job playing the part, but he didn't have the Colonel's build. Tom Hanks needed to be a bit more pear-shaped to give proper representation to The Colonel.

Chapter Eleven

The Nite-Liters, New Birth & The Main Ingredient

Larry Douglas was right, the day RCA had hired me, he told Harvey Fuqua in the hallway; 'you'll be seeing a lot of Tom in the future.' Harvey produced and represented both the Nite-Liters and their vocal complement, New Birth. The instrumental group The Nite-Liters was originally formed by Harvey and Tony Churchill. Before they came to RCA, the group called themselves The Crawlers and were the band behind Alvin Cash. They had a number one record called *'Twine Time'* in 1964. Prior to the Nite-Liters morphing into The New Birth they had several instrumental hits including *'K-Jee'* which went top 20 R&B and Top 40 on the pop charts.

The year was 1974. I lived during the week in New York City and would commute every Friday back to Pittsburgh to spend each weekend with my wife Gloria and our two kids, Jocelyn and Eric. This travel schedule began when RCA moved me to the national albums position in 1971. The weekly commute between Pittsburgh and New York continued for the next 15 years. Four years with RCA and another 11 years running various companies located both in New York City and Pittsburgh. You can only Imagine the relationships, frequent flyer miles, and contacts made based upon my weekly schedule between airports. I became so familiar with all the porters that checked me in and all personnel at the Ambassadors Clubs, that I would get invited to their kids' graduations and weddings. What a routine. 6:00 p.m. every Friday, I would leave from Kennedy airport and fly to Pittsburgh. Every Monday morning while working at RCA and then Buddha Records, I would get up at 5 a.m. Gloria would dress the kids or just wrap them in blankets and we would carry them to the car, most of the time still sleeping. We would then drive to Greater Pittsburgh Airport, and I would catch the 7:10 flight to LaGuardia.

I didn't realize how predictable my routine was until the end of my tenure at RCA. It was a Sunday morning, and I needed to pick up a relative flying into Pittsburgh. I decided to take my kids: Jocelyn, who was six years old, and Eric, who was four. As we pulled up to the airport, the kids looked out the window, pointed to the departure door at the terminal and said, "Look, we're in New York!", and why would they think differently since for years they took me to New York every Monday, then come back from New York every Friday evening to welcome me home.

Throughout all my early years at RCA in I had no permanent residence in Manhattan. Instead, spent my time-sharing apartment space with both Tookie, who had a place in New Rochelle and with Tom Draper at his upper East side three-bedroom apartment on 69th Street. During the time I was living with Draper, most of the R&B artists would visit. Many times, plans and career decisions would be made over drinks. It was a great apartment and meeting place with a great sound system. One evening, Harvey Fuqua stopped by and brought members of the group New Birth with him. Even years after meeting Harvey on that first day at RCA, my respect for the man never changed. He was an R&B legend and a gentleman.

The subject came up about material for the group's forthcoming album, to be titled, *It's Been a Long Time*. New Birth always had good material but were looking for that crossover hit song for both R&B and Pop Radio. If you had that crossover hit record on both formats it was almost a guarantee that you would be heading toward gold album sales. Here in the States, gold albums had to have at least 500,000 units sold and certified by the RIAA. To achieve Platinum status sales had to exceed 1,000,000 units, also certified by the RIAA. The RIAA, Record Industry Association of America was and still is the certification source for all records in those categories.

A friend of mine at Capitol Records had sent me a copy of an album that I loved by a Canadian group called Skylark. I felt this self-titled album was amazing and contained great arrangements and stellar vocal performances. The track, '*Suite for a Lady*' performed by BJ Cook was brilliant. I knew the band did well in Canada but had not caught on here in the states. The album also featured great vocal performances by Donnie Gerrard and exceptional string arrangements by Jimmy Haskel, who I felt was the best string arranger in modern music. The band's leader was David Foster, who in later years became a major force in the music business and a multiple Grammy Winner.

I thought the album was a masterpiece and called Harvey's attention to one special song entitled '*Wildflower*'. Both Harvey and the group agreed, they loved it and decided to record the song. We release it as a featured single from their new album. My only apprehension at the time was competing with the vocal performance by Donny Gerrard. Donny had a world class voice and covering this song would be a daunting task. New Birth covered the song beautifully and it became the group's biggest R&B hit, but only mid-charted on the pop charts. I believe we were still proven right in our assessment of the song. Years later, many other artists performed their own renditions of the song '*Wildflower*'.

The Main Ingredient

I had the pleasure of working with The Main Ingredient on and off from 1970 as an employee at RCA and with my production company Record Logic through 1980. Bert DeCoteaux produced most of the group's albums in the early 70's with R&B Hits off the Album *You've Been My Inspiration*: Including *'I'm So Proud', 'Spinning Around'* and the Donnie McPherson penned song, *'Black Seeds Keep on Growing'*. The original group trio consisted of Donnie, Tony Silvester and Luther Simmons.

The Main Ingredient had two outstanding lead singers during their prime recording years. Donald McPherson and Cuba Gooding Sr. In the summer of 1971, the group's fortunes took a tragic downturn when Donnie passed away from Leukemia. I'll never forget the funeral service held in a small church in Harlem. It was an open casket service and attended by Tom Draper, me, Stu Ginsberg and several others from RCA. Also in attendance were family, musicians, and numerous young ladies who displayed their grief by attempting to jump into the casket with Donnie. Finally, they stationed two pall bearers at each end to keep things respectable. It was truly a remarkable wake for a kind and talented man.

Cuba Gooding Sr. became the lead singer of The Main Ingredient in 1972. He had sung background with the band, knew all the material and had sung Donnie's leads during his Illness. That year, with Cuba singing lead, their single *'Everybody Plays the Fool'* reached the top 5 on Pop and R&B charts and sold over one million copies. Their second million-selling single, *'Just*

Don't Want to Be Lonely', was released two years later and also became a hit single.

After years of solo projects, the band reunited in 1979, and I signed them to my production company, Record Logic. The album was titled *Ready For Love* and was produced by the trio. The single *'Think Positive'* was released, though received only limited airplay.

The name Cuba Gooding may be familiar because his son, Cuba Gooding Jr., is a successful actor who has starred in many movies such as *Jerry Maguire, A Few Good Men,* and *As Good as it Gets*. It is notable how much he resembles his father whenever he appears on screen or TV. I remember his dad, Cuba, Sr., bringing him into my Time Square offices at Record Logic. Cuba Jr. back then was a very personable and extremely energetic kid; the persona didn't seem to change much as he matured into a major film star.

Chapter Twelve

The Pittsburgh Connection

During the four years Frank 'Tookie' Dileo and I worked together in New Your City we both would commute back to our homes in Pittsburgh. Tookie grew up on Larimer Avenue in East Liberty and attended Central Catholic High School. His two wing men were Fat Pat and Skeeter. I grew up in Munhall and briefly attended the Epiphany Seminary then Munhall High School. My two running buddies were Bugsy and Jumby. Tookie started working at Epic records as a promotion man in 1969, I started working in the field for RCA in 1969.

We both were called to NYC to work at RCA in 1970 and we both continued to commute to Pittsburgh on weekends. When we had to stay in New Youk City for the weekend, we shared an apartment in New Rochelle. We were co-captains of the Nippers; our Central Park record industry softball team. We both were young and had great careers while at RCA. And we both ended up moving back to Pittsburgh in the mid 70's. For years after Tookie departed RCA, he worked for Bell Records and the group Tony Orlando and Dawn. I moved back to Pittsburgh to start my own record company. Tookie moved back a year later. We were in a record company Brotherhood.

Tookie, to enhance his income, became 'Took the Book' and being a good friend, I would place all my Sunday morning football bets with 'Took the Book'. One Sunday after the late games were over, I got a call asking how much money I had in hand. Tookie was in a jam for getting creative by trying to hit the middle, or sometimes called jakeing a bet, and not turning in the book when neither side wins. Which in this case, went drastically awry. I went to the bank early Monday morning and pulled out the two thousand dollars that I had for emergencies. I believed this to be the definition of an emergency and gave Tookie the money. Yet, for some reason a week later, his house burnt down. Good news, no one was home.

Steve Greenberg, Frank O'Donnell, Cossie, and Tookie either talking to a radio station or taking a bet?
Photo Credit Nick Sangiamo

Tookie would later return to New York and make a major comeback in the camp of Michael Jackson.

Let us jump from our early days at RCA for a moment up to the year 1979. My partner Marc Kreiner and I signed Chic to Atlantic in late1977 and by 1979 we were working on our third Chic hit record with Atlantic, the record was *La Freak*, which went to Number one on the Billboard chart selling close to 5 million singles. Tookie also moved back to New York City and became the head of Promotion for Epic Records. This is now ten years after he started with Epic back in 1969. Once in the saddle again, Tookie didn't waste any time establishing Epic Records as the Star of the CBS record group. Under his promotional guidance he launched the hit record making careers of; Meat Loaf, Gloria Estefan, Quiet Riot, Reo Speedwagon, and Cyndi Lauper.

Frank's entrance back to Epic also came during Michael's *Off The Wall* release. Michael Jackson was already a well-known child star with The Jackson Five, long before both of his multi-platinum albums, *Off the Wall,* and his biggest selling album *Thriller,* were released. For the duration of the Jackson Five's long musical timeline, with multiple albums, and constant touring, Michael and his brothers were managed by their taskmaster father, Joe Jackson. Michael as a solo artist started hitting his prime with the release of *Off the Wall*, which contained the hit singles; *'Don't Stop Till You Get Enough'* and *'Rock with You'*. Successful singles consistently contribute to album sales, each time a new MJ single was released from the album, sales would once again take off. A year after the release of *Off the Wall*, and over three million album sales later, Frank asked me to meet him at his home in Wellsville, Ohio, just across the Southwestern Pennsylvania border. The drive to his home was only 45 minutes from downtown Pittsburgh, Tookie liked the privacy rural living provided.

We were sitting on his back porch, and he pulled out a contract, which appeared to me to be about an inch thick. Tookie told me that Michael thought his latest album *Off the Wall* didn't do as well as he expected, even though sales at that point were over three million copies. Any normal artist would be thrilled with sales of that magnitude; then again, every artist was not Michael Jackson. I asked Tookie about the contract.

He explained, "Well, about a month ago Michael was in my office with his attorney, John Branca, who at that time had stepped in as another interim manager for Michael. It seemed Michael was having problems with his father Joe, long before the release of *Off the Wall,* and Michael was looking for a change in management. He had several interim managers after his dad, but Michael still wasn't satisfied." Tookie said he reassured Michael this current album was going to continue to sell with the groundwork the company had laid so far." And then he told Michael, "I will guarantee you; we will at least double the sales on the new album, *Thriller*. This is my promise to you."

He took a breath before continuing, "Michael seemed to like my attitude and told Walter Yetnikoff, the President of EPIC Records, that he wanted me to be his manager. That's what this contract is about. So, the contract states I will be his manager and get a nice percentage of all record sales as well as a piece of his live performances. What do you think I should do?"

I thought to myself, if Tookie signs that contract, it would be like receiving the winning ticket in a super lottery. It would make my friend, "Took the Book" an instant millionaire many times over.

Tookie then told me, "This will be an entire life change, I'd have to travel the world with this 'kid', and I don't know if I want that much action"

I said "Took, all that action, are you kidding? Action is your middle name, remember you were "Took the Book" only a few years ago and now you have a whole new, bright, promising world ahead."

Frank "Tookie" Dileo, took the deal and for the next three years managed that 'kid', Michael Jackson. Tookie's promise to Michael came true, as sales did more than double with *Thriller*, reportedly selling over six million units during the first two years of its initial release. Some current reports say the *Thriller* album to date has sold over sixty million albums world-wide. Now that's what I call a hit album.

It was the early 80's. I was in Los Angeles visiting Tookie at his home in Encino. Michael had a home only a few blocks away. Sales on his album were phenomenal, and Michel wanted to show his appreciation and offered to buy Tookie a Royals Royce of his choice. I asked Frank why he didn't go for the Corniche Convertible. He said he didn't want to seem greedy and besides, he was a family man, so just asked for The Silver Spur.

I was standing in Frank's driveway late one Saturday morning when Michael pulled up in his Rolls. It was a beautiful new Corniche Convertible. My used 528I BMW looked out of place next to the two new Rolls Royce's. Michael stepped out of the car walked across the driveway, and in a soft voice said, "Hi Frank, nice car."

I'd seen Michael in concert, courtesy of tickets from Tookie, but never saw him up close. I didn't realize how much taller he was in person, not knowing if it was the shoes or just standing next to Tookie. Frank said, "you remember Tom", Michael turned and said a quick but cordial, 'Hi Tom'. My guess was he probably didn't have a clue as to who I was. He then headed into Frank's back yard and into the cabana house next to Frank's swimming pool.

I said to Tookie, "It looks like you have a meeting, so I'll head out."

Frank shook his head and grinned, "No, hang out a while. There's no meeting. Michael does this all the time; He comes over, walks back, and goes into the cabana. He then turns up the air conditioning to full, lights up the fireplace, he grabs a book off the shelf, then reclines on the couch and pulls up the Afghan and reads for about a half hour. He then gets up, turns off the air, shuts off the fireplace, folds the Afghan, puts the book back, then comes into the house and gets into a pillow battle with Dominic and Balinda. After about fifteen minutes, and after the kids are wound up, he says bye to me and the Chief and then leaves." (Dominic and Belinda are Tookie's kids, and his wife Linda has always been lovingly referred to as "Chief").

During this brief encounter with Michael, I thought to myself, the Michael I just encountered did not seem to match the character or villainized profile of a child abuser, often described in the news. I felt bad for him, considering how the pace of show business operates, the judgements, the constant living under a microscope. And there was Michael, the youngest of five, continuously on the road most of his life. It seemed he never had a shot of living a normal childhood.

Tookie told me, the 'kid' was Ok, and that was cool with me.

Chapter Thirteen
Best of Nashville
Dolly Parton

RCA Records dominated country music in Nashville for decades with a roster of major country artists. The label's success dates to the fifties, and has continued for decades. When I worked for RCA through independent distribution in the late 60's, I remember going weekly to the local country stations, retail stores, and wholesale one-stops, delivering promotional copies of at least five new releases just on the RCA label. It seemed like Jim Reeves, Eddy Arnold, Hank Snow, Dotty West, Waylon Jennings, Porter Wagoner and Dolly Parton would come out with a new single every month and almost every one of those singles would hit the country charts.

In the late 60's, Dolly teamed up with Porter Wagoner. Porter was already an established artist on the label and invited her to be his partner on his successful TV show. Her popularity took off and because of her success and a recommendation from Porter, RCA decided to sign her to a solo recording contract. Her duos with Porter generated over 20 country hit singles as well as a dozen hit albums. Several successful but turbulent years later, rumors started in

Nashville about friction between the two regarding artistic control and how her business was handled. Dolly had a mind of her own and was ahead of her time when it came to standing up for her own control of her music and artistic direction in her life.

A good case in point for her independence was around the same time she wrote the song 'Jolene' she also wrote a song entitled '*I Will Always Love You*'. Elvis heard '*I Will Always Love You*', felt it was a hit. Enter Colonel Tom Parker, you remember the Colonel from Chapter Eleven, he approached Dolly and told her Elvis wanted to record the song. Dolly was thrilled at the offer. Historically, when a major artist wants to record and release one of your songs, the value of that copyright for the writer and publishers would dramatically increase. For an unknown song writer this meant money in the bank and a major boost in notoriety.

The deal was almost consummated until The Colonel told her that part of the deal involved Dolly giving him 50% ownership of her song. If you were an unknown songwriter, this opportunity would be extremely attractive and an acceptable compromise. Dolly, however, having had chart successes on her own, told the Colonel, 'No Thank You.' The song later became a number one record sung by Whitney Houston, and Dolly retained 100% control of copyright ownership. Dolly's realization of self-worth and independence likely caused Dolly's separation from Porter Wagner.

It also led to her tremendous success in every facet of the entertainment industry.

When I went to work directly for RCA, first as a regional representative then in New York City as head of promotion, I had the pleasure of meeting a lot of famous country artists. In the early 70's RCA had success in crossing over records from the country charts to the pop charts. Most country artists felt that having a hit record on the country charts was good but limited to one group of fans. If they were lucky enough and their music had mainstream appeal, and received airplay on both country and pop radio, their careers would take off exponentially. Thanks to exposure on multiple radio formats. Jerry Reed, with his hit single *'Amos Moses'*, Charlie Pride, *'Kiss an Angel Good Morning'*, and Dolly Parton with *'Jolene'*. Were prime examples of crossover hit single.

To me, Dolly Parton was a unique artist that exemplified both charm and kindness, when combined with her obvious attractiveness projected an aura of beauty. My introduction to Dolly took place in 1973. I was the Director of National Album Promotion based in New York City, and Dolly's latest single, *'Jolene',* had made the jump from Country radio to mainstream pop radio. Elroy "The Country Son" Kahanek was RCA's Director of Country Music Promotion based in Nashville. Elroy, when he would talk to you on the phone would start of by saying, in a long drawn-out accent…"Son"… therefore I would always refer to Elroy as "The Country Son". He always told me that Dolly is one of the best singers and songwriters in Nashville as well as one of our coolest young artists in the RCA family. Most of the legendary country artists on the RCA roster were at least fifteen to twenty years older than Dolly, so in essence, being as successful as she was and in her early 20's was notable.

Dolly was in New Your City to do press interviews and was staying at the Plaza Hotel. My Boss, Frank Mancini, asked me to visit Dolly and give her an update on her album, *Jolene*, the same title as the hit single. I arrived at the hotel, called her room and she said she was expecting me and had just got off the phone with Frank. Her suite had a small hallway leading into a sitting room with an entrance into a large bedroom. Elroy was on the money when he told me Dolly was one of the coolest people in Nashville. During our initial conversation, I learned that we were of the same age, and both graduated from high school in 1964. After about a half hour of talking about her album, life in Nashville, and me living in The Big Apple, she told me Frank and Mel Ilberman, the head of Business affairs, were also meeting with her that morning to talk over a contract issue.

It seemed like only moments later that the phone rang, Frank was on the line with Dolly. They were in the lobby, and on their way up to the room. Dolly looked at me and said in a half whispering, yet provocative country voice, "Tom, I've got a great idea. Leave the hotel door just a little bit open, and you and me will jump into bed and pull the covers over us so just our heads are showing. Then when they come a-knocking, we won't answer the door, they'll let themselves in, cause I'm expecting them, and when they come in and see us, well just throw off the covers."

I immediately said, "I don't think that is such a great idea."

Dolly laughingly said, "Come on, it will be fun to see their reaction and we will have all of our clothes on so what could go wrong."

Moments later we were in that king sized bed with covers up to our necks, both looking through two large open doors into the sitting room. There was a knock on the door which, by design, was left slightly ajar. I heard Frank call my name. Dolly whispered, "Don't say a word." Within seconds both Frank and Mel were standing in the bedroom doorway, staring at two heads, one of a gorgeous blond and one of a long-haired hippy and, hopefully still employed, promotion man. Frank had daggers coming out of his eyes and Mel looked like he was having a heart attack.

Dolly threw off the covers and said "Surprise! Great seeing you guys!" This was the first time I ever saw my boss speechless. The two of them just shook their heads and started laughing. It was at that point I thought to myself, this girl can take over the world if she wished to do so. And the music and media business! She did just that!

In the years after my meeting with her at the Plaza Hotel in 1973, she went on to be nominated for just about every award known to the record industry and walked away with over ten Grammy awards as well as ten CMAs, (Country Music Awards). I recently read a story about the top thirty best-selling country artists in the history of the music industry. The only two top country recording artists who both sold over 100 million records were Gath Brooks and Dolly Parton. God Bless Dolly, she deserves all she has worked for.

Meetings in Nashville

Dandy Don Whittemore III, Don "Captain Spacy" Delacy, Rob Hegal, Lou Galliani, and Tom Cossie

Chapter Fourteen
Shock Jock Don Imus
1,200 Hamburgers to Go

Cleveland Radio in the late 60's was a strong rock and roll town as well as being a major music breakout market for new music. WIXY was the number one pop station, WMMS was the hard rock king of the airwaves, and WGAR was the middle of the road station that hosted the originator of Shock Jock Radio, the controversial, Don Imus.

The *Imus In The Morning* radio program was heard on the airwaves for over 30 years, beginning in 1967 at WGAR in Cleveland and then moving to New York City in 1971. As the RCA regional promotion rep for the Cleveland market, I would listen to his radio show driving up from Pittsburgh and often wondered how he got away with some of the comments he made and live radio skits he performed. *Imus In The Morning* created an array of fictitious characters like The Reverend Billy Sol Hargus. Another of his infamous characters was a very official sounding Sargent Kirkland. The Sargent would call up a local restaurant and place an order for

1,200 Hamburgers to go saying his troops were on a special assignment and needed lunch. They wanted to pick up the burgers in two hours. Panic would ensue as the employee would check with his manager to see if they had enough buns, etc.

The comedic dialogue and banter between Don and the shocked order taker would go back and forth with Don pushing the limits, changing the order request for 350 with tomatoes and mayo, 400 with mustard and onion but no lettuce. Then say, no, 300 with mustard and onion but add lettuce. By the end of the order—if the store owner hadn't hung up by then—Imus would close with the final request of 900 chocolate shakes and three hundred cokes. This was one of many live on-air phone calls he would make to unsuspecting business owners or event schedulers. One time he tried to order from Hertz rental cars in Indianapolis one of their high-performance Mustangs, saying he was going to enter it in a national racing event. He wanted the Hertz rental office to give him a special rate because he only needed to put 500 miles on the car.

Don and I became friends during our Cleveland days. When I moved to New York City in 1970, as the National Albums Promotion Director, my thoughts would always return to those fun and entertaining radio days. When Don decided to move to NYC in 1971, we stayed in touch. As it turned out he signed a big contract with NBC Radio who wanted to bring the Imus In The Morning event into the Big Apple. At that time RCA was a division of NBC which owned radio property WNBC. The Imus Shock Jock show took the city by storm. One evening I took Don out for a few drinks to ask him if he ever thought of making an album out of some of his skits. It was my considered opinion that among all the characters he portrayed there was enough material to do at least two albums.

Rocco Lagenestra was the President of RCA at the time and my relationship with him was good. We had great success with Harry Nilsson, and I shared dinner with Rocco and Harry on several occasions. I felt comfortable in planting the seed that Imus wanted RCA to release some of his material. Since we had an A&R department that was responsible for singing artists, I didn't want to appear I was going over anyone's head by going directly to the president. To avoid the conundrum, I told Rocco that Don and I had been friends for years and he asked me to arrange a dinner with Rocco.

As it turned out, Mr. Lagenestra, as well as all the senior executives at the corporation, listened to *Imus In The Morning* on their commutes driving into the city. You have a lot of time to listen to the radio during a traffic commute into the city from any of New York City's upscale neighboring communities. I set up the dinner and Don's pitch to Rocco went well. At that meeting I mentioned one of our staff producers with a great sense of humor named Pete Spargo. Pete was the producer who would bail me out on a future dilemma which will occur in a future chapter. I thought Pete would be the perfect fit to produce and deal with our super star radio jock/soon to be recording artist.

Within the next few weeks, A&R had a two album agreement ready for Don to sign. Since both RCA and WNBC were under the same ownership the deal was consummated with little drama or crazy negotiation tactics.

Over the next year Pete recorded both albums for Don. One titled '1200 Hamburgers to Go' and the second album was 'One Sacred Chicken to Go'. I can't remember if either of those albums sold well. I'm sure because of his radio popularity they at least broke even.

Don Imus was a hoot, a friend, and I always enjoyed running into him at various bars in NYC. We both enjoyed a few drinks and as each evening wore on, I couldn't figure out how he could stay up until all hours then be sharp to do his daily morning show. Then the solution to the quandary blazed like a noonday sun. Don, like a lot of my artist and music business friends, got heavily into the Peruvian marching dust, more commonly known as cocaine or blow. I was lucky because for some reason my body responded differently to blow. After a long day and soaking down about four or five rusty nails or numerous tequila shots I was ready to head home. If I did drugs on top of drinking, especially cocaine became lethargic instead of amped up.

Smoking a doobie or taking a few hits from a bong was more in line for my evening relaxation.

One evening after the release of '*1200 Hamburgers to Go*', I ran into Don at a bar next to Rockefeller Center. We had a few laughs, I explained to Don most of his album sales came from his radio name recognition, the traditional way of exposure was airplay on as many radio stations as possible. If you think about it, though, how many other disc jockeys are going to play another disc jockeys record. Surely not Howard Stern. Don seemed to understand and didn't seem too bothered by the lack of traditional airplay.

The next morning, I was back in my office at 8:30. Being a morning person I always liked to get a jump on the day before everyone started to file in around 10. It was about 10:30 when my intercom rang. It was Rocco. He said, "Tom, tell me it's not true about the TV and stereo system you gave Don Imus. I was listening to him this morning and I just got off the phone with my boss at corporate, he also said he heard Imus say, 'I want to thank Tom Cossie, my friend and promotion man at RCA, for the new TV and Stereo. He really knows how to take care of business.' He then proceeded to play one of Nilssons records."

I told Rocco, "You know Don's crazy, and I would never offer payola. Even if I did, especially for Don, it sure wouldn't be a TV or Stereo." This event was embarrassing but was never mentioned again by either me or Rocco. That is until I saw Don about a week later. When he saw me, he started laughing like he pulled a fast one, and said, "Cossie, that was good for your image!"

I realized, it was no great shock or wonder he got kicked off the air so many times.

In thinking back, I have to say that cocaine, among all the drugs that were consumed in the sixties and seventies, was perhaps the most disastrous of all career wrecking drugs. Being around artists and performers who are always on the public stage, you realize adulation weighs heavily on human acceptance, emotions and decision making. Drugs to these artists seem to be the panacea that makes reality more acceptable. I've seen young performers step onto stadium stages in front of tens of thousands of cheering fans. This experience can be overwhelming, and the reality is, many turn to drugs to cope with the pressure. Not everyone is equipped mentally to be praised as a deity. On or off the stage.

I came across this article which I thought was apropos. It's a piece printed by Source Guardian and is titled, *Drugs in the Music Business.*

Why Is Drug Use So Popular in the Music Industry?

Despite the glamorous lives portrayed in the media, entertainers are exposed to pressures many of us never experience. These factors can contribute to drug use.

The fast-paced lifestyle of touring and performing can lead to burnout or exhaustion, making it difficult for musicians to cope without using drugs or alcohol as a crutch.

What Are the Risk Factors for Substance Misuse Among Musicians?

• Access to money makes it easier for them to obtain drugs

- Lack of education about the dangers of drug use.

- Peer pressure from other entertainers.

- Stress related to fame.

- Boredom due to lack of meaningful activities.

- Loneliness due to being away from family and friends.

- Physical pain caused by performing strenuous activities such as dancing or singing.

- Mental health issues such as depression or anxiety.

- Easy access due to being surrounded by people who may be involved in the drug trade.

- Trauma such as physical or sexual abuse.

- Article- Courtesy of Guardian News and Media, LTD.

This Chapter about Don Imus is not intended to preach about the use of drugs. However, I'm positive that cocaine caused a lot of unnecessary hardships over his career and has had a crippling effect on many artists, their vocal quality and eventual career demise.

Chapter Fifteen

Brian Auger and His Oblivion Express

Many may not be familiar with Brian Auger or for that matter, Steampacket, one of Brian's initial blues and jazz bands from the British music scene of 1965. Brian Auger played my favorite keyboard instrument, the Hammond B3 organ in the band Steampacket, which included notable members such as Long John Baldry, Vic Briggs, Julie Driscoll, and Rod Stewart. Each of these individuals would go on to have distinguished careers in the music industry, with varying degrees of prominence, Rod obviously being the most notable. It is believed that Brian was greatly inspired by renowned jazz artists like Les McCann and Eddie Harris. Their rendition of the song *'Compared to What'* appeared to significantly influence the direction of Brian's subsequent projects.

Brian's recording career with RCA began in 1970 with the release of his first album of eight projects up through 1975. In Music Business Stories, many tales are told about great artistry, who makes it to the top of the charts, and those who with equal or greater talent are challenged to ever see record chart activity. The 1973 release of Brian Auger's Oblivion Express, *Closer To It,* is an excellent example of this fight for chart notoriety.

In 1973 Billy Bass was RCA's National Album Promotion Manager, Michael "The Rookie" Abramson was head of RCA's Product Management Team, and I had recently been named RCA Senior VP of Promotion.

Cleveland, one of the nation's top breakout markets, was a great place to launch this project. Billy Bass was a former star radio Disc Jockey on the number one Cleveland rock station, WMMS. Michael was one of the best promotion men to have previously worked in the Cleveland market and Cleveland was also one of the first cities I worked when I was first hired by RCA in 1969. This should have been the recipe for success since the Oblivion Express album *Closer To It,* was considered one of the most commercial Auger albums to date. The mission was now to launch this project.

Michael Abramson communicated to Violini, RCA's sales manager, his strategy to promote this album to garner sales support. Consequently, Bass and Abramson formulated a comprehensive plan which included radio promotion on WMMS, local television coverage and coordination with The Music Grotto for retail follow up. There was also a prominent full-length billboard on Euclid Avenue, one of the city's main streets.

Billy Bass, Michael Abramson, and Dominic Violini, RCA's Cleveland sales manager, were overseeing the event. They are pictured between Brian Auger on the left and Tom Cossie on the far right after a concert at the Agora Night Club in Cleveland.

They met with WMMS and demonstrated their commitment on both local and national levels, which led to WMMS's willingness to support the project. Radio stations typically hesitated to play a record that had not been proven successful. While no station wanted to be the first to play it, once the record gained popularity, every station sought recognition for breaking the artist. WMMS, noted for being on the cutting edge of breaking artists, was the first to play it and especially deserved the credit due. This album sold well in that market. Cleveland is known as a prominent city for Rock & Roll and houses the Rock & Roll Hall of Fame.

In the early seventies, the radio disc jockey and programming team at WMMS-FM "The Buzzard," including Billy Bass, Kid Leo, Martin Perlich, Shana, David Spero, and the dynamic WMMS program director, John Gorman, played a major role in establishing Cleveland's reputation as leader in rock music. Ahmet Ertegun, the founder of Atlantic Records and The Rock & Roll Hall of Fame, likely considered WMMS as a contributing factor when selecting Cleveland as the site for the Rock & Roll Hall of Fame, which opened in 1995.

This Brian Auger Oblivion Express campaign featured two large album covers painted on The Music Grotto's building. This key retailer also committed to in-store play. Bass and Abramson wrote radio and TV scripts for WMMS, with Cleveland's well-known radio voice Billy Bass as the announcer.

The RCA staff delivered an excellent performance, delivering a high-quality album campaign that attained significant positions on the Jazz, R&B, Billboard, Cash Box, and Record Worlds charts, although it did not reach its full hit record potential. Nevertheless, Brian Auger, as the leader of a predominantly instrumental band, earned considerable respect within the music community. In later years, three of his former band members from The Oblivion Express formed The Average White Band.

Chapter Sixteen

Harry - Ringo and John

Beatlemania exploded into the pop music world in 1962 and by the mid-60's the British Invasion was in full swing. Back then the music of my identity was more related to bands and songs like The Coasters, *'Searchin'* or *'Poison Ivy'*, or the rhythmic music of *'Soul Man'*, or *'You Got Me Hummin'* by Sam and Dave. The Beatles ...*'Love, Love, Me Do'*, or *'A Hard Day's Night'* were not selections on my dance card. If the Beatles were giving a free concert one side of town and The Coasters on the other side, I would be spending time with *'Charlie Brown'* and the Coasters.

As a dance and R&B music record collector, I did not feel the vibe of Beatlemania. Most kids in my age group, or younger, did not share my musical opinion and were over the top for The Beatles. Back in my younger days, I thought their song writing was more prolific than their talent as performers. Back in the mid-sixties I thought the Beatles and Stones were just British Wana-be American R&B artists. They often times would cover R&B songs or try to be more soulful than they were, though the Stones were probably the best equipped to be credible.

Harry Nilsson in the early 70's became an integral part in the London circle of music artists, producers, and friends. Trident and Abby Road Studios were the creative meeting grounds where the music was recorded, and where most of the artists and producers networking took place. It was commonplace for producers like Richard Perry and Derek Taylor to collaborate and integrate the top recording artists in each other's recording secessions.

One example of this inner comradery was in 1972, when Ringo played drums on Harry's album *Son of Schmilsson*. So, it was no surprise when Harry was recording or working on a film in NYC that friends like Ringo or John Lennon would take part in his recording process.

During my RCA NYC days I met both Ringo and John Lennon. Ringo in 1972 and John in 1974. In late '72, Harry was working together with Ringo on a rock and roll spoof film called 'Son of Dracula'. Harry starred as Count Downe, the son of the recently murdered Count Dracula, and Ringo Starr played the role of Merlin the Magician, the Dracula family's trusted sorcerer. The movie was released in 1974 and though conceptually interesting, received negative reviews from film critics. Though Harry portrayed the son of a vampire to the teeth, and Ringo did wear the sorcerer's hat well, their fun filled spoof performances didn't seem to move the film critics opinions.

My first meeting with Ringo took place on a cold New York City winter day just before Christmas. Christmas in New York was like no other. All the street scenes you see in the movies are true, horse drawn carriage rides in central park, the air permeated by the smell of roasted chestnuts provided by street side venders, and festive holiday decorations draped the streets and avenues in all directions. Fifth Ave was my favorite shopping location and Tiffany's was my all-time favorite store, especially at Christmas. Most of the high-end expensive diamond enhanced jewelry was located on the main floor. My hidden Tiffany treasures were located on the second floor. It took a lot of self-control to walk past the sparkling display cases to the rear of the store then take the elevator to the second floor.

Right around the corner of the elevator, there were two large sales tables adorned with Christmas decorations. Those two tables were also loaded with hundreds of small yet beautiful and practical everyday items. This was the era of rotary phones and there was an item to make dialing easier by using a sterling silver phone dialer. They also had on display sterling silver key chains, book markers, money clips, as well as my favorite, the sterling silver clad toothpaste key. Each of these items were strategically displayed on top of a small blue silk sack, positioned inside a beautiful three-inch by three-inch blue Tiffany box. If this total package wasn't special enough, each item sold for only $25.00.

Having completed this Christmas shopping trip in record time, I promptly exited Tiffany's with two bags filled with elegantly wrapped gifts in their signature blue boxes. I couldn't wait to get back to RCA's headquarters and studios.

The offices were all but closed for the Christmas vacation break, I had my bags packed, my company car in the garage next to the studios awaiting the 8-hour drive back to Pittsburgh. The Christmas break in the record business was always a welcome time ending a hectic year. And this year, I looked forward to spending some extended time with my family.

I held both of those large Tiffany shopping bags with one hand and hailed a cab with the other. As luck would have it, a Checker cab pulled up. It was always a plus when a Checker arrived, especially when you had packages in hand. That type of cab had a large flat space in front of the seats which provided an ample area to accommodate multiple suitcases or in this case, shopping bags. I asked the driver to take a slightly longer route to the RCA's 44th Street Studio entrance. We headed down 5th Avenue then went west across 42nd Street and across Time Square. I wanted to have a last seasonal glimpse of our center city Christmas decorations. We then proceeded up 8th Avenue, before turning east on 44th St, to the RCA Street Studio entrance. The cab pulled up and dropped me off just ahead of a large black limousine with dark tinted windows. Grabbing my shopping bags, I made my way to the studio entrance. Just before entering the building, I heard a familiar voice call out, "Hey Cossie, come on over."

I was on a mission to pick up some paperwork at my office and start my journey to Pittsburgh while there was still daylight. But the voice was Harry Nilsson's. I turned to face the limousine, and he waved at me out of a large half opened, blacked out rear window, to come over to the car. For a fleeting moment I thought, 'Oh No, this may present a serious delay in my planned exit from the city.' It was however the Christmas season, and I wanted to wish one of my favorite artists, and friend, a Merry Christmas. I walked over to the car, Harry popped open the limo door and I jumped into the private back seat area, facing the rear window. This Limousine had four plush seats, two forward and two back, facing each other with a small table in the center. I placed my two Tiffany shopping bags on the seat next to me, turned around, and sat down facing two friendly but somewhat glazed faces. Those being of Harry, wearing his favorite hat, and Ringo Starr.

Harry, I knew well. I'd spent numerous evenings over cocktails and had eventful, fun adventures, including the year of The Industrial Diamond Caper. This was the first time I met Ringo in person. In years to come I would realize Ringo was Harry's long-time friend and even helped Harry design his new home just west of Beverly Hills.

Harry was wearing the cool hat he always wore. Ringo, though not wearing a hat, I pictured sporting that magician's hat he wore as Merlin in their Son of Dracula film. Being parked in front of the studio entrance, I assumed they were either going in to work on some recording or were just leaving the studio. On a small table between us I noticed what looked like a substantial mound of cocaine, directly next to a tightly rolled up one-hundred-dollar bill. Personally, I was more of a drinker, though, with friends, I would occasionally take a few hits of weed off a bong after a long day at the office. I never really got into blow, which for years was the drug of choice in the music business. As mentioned earlier, when I did take a few hits, I found that cocaine had a reverse effect on me. Instead of getting amped up, this drug made me lethargic. Knowing I had a long drive home, I politely declined their offer of hospitality. After a few moments of well-wishing and talking about the film and my planned journey home, I wished them Merry Christmas.

Just as I was making my exit, I paused and said, "I have a small gift that I'd like to give you both." I thought, 'Ok, these two stars would never use a sterling phone dialer, or have need for a money clip, or small keychain, but most assuredly they brushed their teeth. The sterling toothpaste key would be the ticket.' Those keys were always one of the most popular of my Tiffany purchases, even though most people, upon first gaze, didn't have any idea of what this gift was. Since I packed the shopping bags, I knew the toothpaste keys were on top. The toothpaste key was such a cool gift, a two-inch circular rod with the top hollowed out to accommodate the bottom ridge of a toothpaste tube. Sliding that ridge in the key slot, and with a quick turn of the key, more toothpaste was effortlessly available. What a brilliant invention. I reached in the bag and handed over two iconic classic blue Tiffany boxes. They both looked pleasantly surprised. Harry immediately pulled on the blue ribbon, opened the box, removed the small silk bag, and took out the polished toothpaste key. With one quick motion, he leaned forward to the small table and filled the valley of the key with white powder, then ran his index finger over the top of the channel creating a smooth uniform line of blow in the key's cavity. In one equally quick motion, he held the key up to his nose and the white powder disappeared. Harry then turned towards Ringo said, "Holy Shit, I didn't know Tiffany's made these."

On that note I said, "guys, Merry Christmas and Happy New Year. I got a long drive ahead."

John Lennon In the House

In the Spring of 1974, I had recently been appointed Senior Vice President of Promotion and was now had a new home in that corner office once occupied by Frank Mancini. Harry and John Lennon were working on an album entitled *Pussy Cats* which would contain a single entitled 'Many Rivers to Cross'. Harry loved this song and some months before they started recording, he came into the office and played for me the Jimmy Cliff original. I thought it was a great choice, and I knew Harry would do a great job on the vocal. At the time, I would have bet this forthcoming album would be a hit. Harry and John had an all-star musical cast for this album; Klaus Voormann, the legendary bass player who performed on all of Harry's previous hit albums, drums and percussion were by Keith Moon, Jimmy Keltner and Ringo Starr. My calculation was, with all this talent and superstar John Lennon producing the album, this was going to be a slam dunk at radio and be a chart blockbuster.

The album recording started in California, but due to excessive drug use and minimal creative progress, recording was moved to our NYC studios on 44th St. The thought being a less Wild West influence would deliver a more productive recording outcome. Since the executives at RCA occupied most of the floors above our New York City studios, a 'let's keep a closer eye on the kids' approach was taken.

Unlike most of the west coast studios where you could smoke a joint behind the control board or dice up some blow on the open edge of the control board, the RCA studios were not considered drug friendly locations. When artists needed to go out on break, it usually was into a tinted glass windowed limousine parked out on the street.

Harry Nilsson and John Lennon were thrown out of the Troubadour club in West Hollywood, for heckling a performance by the Smothers Brothers, 12th March 1974. Wild and Crazy times (Photo by Maureen Donaldson/ Getty Images)

The only time I remember any drugs being used in those studio rooms was one time when John Denver and I shared a joint in one of the smaller vacant mixing rooms during a lunch break, out of sight of Denver's producer Milt Oken. Other than that, No Bueno, when it came to drug use in the building and the recording studios. RCA had the image of being square and oftentimes out of touch with the permissive artist community. The corporate image was always the forefront. I learned this lesson firsthand when I was fired from RCA a year later.

Although artists typically had control over album titles, song selections, and music direction, the marketing department intervened and convinced Harry and the album's producer John Lennon that their original title, *Strange Pussies,* would not be suitable. They changed the title to *Pussy Cats* despite some resistance.

One late afternoon toward the end of one of the sessions, Harry and John made their way up to the 10th floor and into my office. They both looked like they hadn't slept for a few days and had on a cocaine buzz. This visual was enhanced by some excess white powder running along both of their noses and upper lips. For a moment it almost seemed funny and reminded me of a John Belushi cocaine skit he did on Saturday Night Live, with powder sugar surrounding his nose and mouth. I was glad they came up the studio elevator in the back of the building, and it was late in the afternoon when most of the office personnel were gone for the day.

Harry brought with him a tape track of '*Many Rivers to Cross'*. He wound it onto my tape deck. The track sounded great up to the moment when Harry started to sing. I was taken back in disbelief as this once velvety voice, sounded like sandpaper rubbing against my ears. His voice sounded terrible. Even more disturbing was both Harry's and John's reaction to Harry's performance. For some reason they both thought he sounded Ok. I shut off the tape and said,

"Harry, I think you need to give the voice a rest. If you don't, you could do permanent damage trying to sing in this condition." Besides both guys looked like the buzz had worn off and sleep was the only solution. Not just because Lennon, only seconds before, leaned back onto my office wall knocking down a gold Guess Who album. The saddest part of this visit was, as bad as Harry's voice sounded, he thought he sounded good. With all the time I was around Harry, we drank a lot, and Harry did like blow, but this time I think the cocaine had taken its toll. I don't know how they finished that album, but they did, and *Pussy Cats* was released some months later. Though the album wasn't a complete disaster, it received little airplay, and only mid chart status on Billboard and the other trade magazines.

Chapter Seventeen

John Denver

A Walk Down Country Road

Of all the artists I met over the years, John Denver stood out as one of the most unique. He was an enigma wrapped in simplicity. His singing voice, long blond hair, horn-rimmed granny glasses, his communication style, smile, lyrics, delivery, performance, and personality, if you knew one part of John, you knew them all. He was, without question, one of the most iconic folk singer-songwriters of our generation. A pleasure to work with. A joy to promote. A true musical artist, someone who loved their craft so deeply, he'd joyfully perform for one person, ten people, or ten thousand—anytime, anywhere. That was John Denver.

John's early career engagements with The New Christy Minstrels and The Chad Mitchell Trio gave him a solid musical/performance foundation and ultimately led him to launch a solo career in 1969. RCA Records was lucky he made that leap. Over the next five years, John Denver sold over thirty million records for RCA, his first breakout single came in 1971: *'Take Me Home, Country Roads'* from the *Poems, Prayers & Promises* album. That song marked the beginning of a platinum-studded career with unforgettable hits like *'Rocky Mountain High'*, *'Sunshine on My Shoulders'*, *'Thank God I'm a Country Boy'*, and *'Annie's Song'.*

A constant in John's career was his longtime producer, Milt Okun. Milt was seemingly always around our New York offices, and rightly so, he was a pivotal figure in John's success. After producing the Chad Mitchell Trio, he worked on one of John's earliest songwriting successes, *'Leaving on a Jet Plane'*, which became a number one hit for Peter, Paul and Mary. So, it came as no surprise that Milt would also produce Denver's remarkable run of hits in the years to come.

Interestingly, despite being such a prolific writer, with hundreds of recorded songs, John didn't write *'Take Me Home, Country Roads'*. It was penned by his friend Bill Danoff. The track has since become something of a state anthem for West Virginia, regularly sung at sporting events and public gatherings. In 1976, John returned the favor by having Milt produce *'Afternoon Delight',* another Danoff hit, this time with Bill and his wife Taffy's group, the Starland Vocal Band.

As many artists do, John eventually sought to create his own record label. Often these vanity labels were more ego than enterprises, and they were usually supported by the parent company. Jefferson Airplane had Grunt Records under RCA, The Rolling Stones had their imprint with Atlantic, and John Denver launched Windsong

Records, distributed by RCA. It was on Windsong that John introduced the Starland Vocal Band to the world.

Now, *'Take Me Home, Country Roads'* wasn't an overnight success. We had some pressing issues at the plant that initially produced defective singles. John's new manager, Jerry Weintraub, wasn't pleased. He put pressure on our VP, the ever-steady Frank Mancini, demanding a full national reservice. Frank, being friends with Jerry and his then-wife, actress Jane Morgan, took it seriously. He not only committed to a reservice of the single but launched an all-out promotional push. That push meant sending our National Singles Promotion Director, Frank "Tookie" DiLeo, to hit the road. I remember Tookie telling me, "Mancini told me to hit the road with this single and don't come back until you've got airplay."

Tookie started pulling strings, landing new record plays in Denver and Cleveland, though he knew he needed a deeper regional campaign. Just three weeks prior, he'd been in Marietta, Georgia, an influential radio market and Atlanta suburb. Frank had attended a weekly radio and promotion gathering hosted by "The Mouth of the South," Jimmy "Ol' Bear" Davenport. It was never quite clear whether the Ol' Bear was the program director at WFOM, an independent promoter, or both. What was clear was his ability to break new records. His home meetings and weekly parties were both notorious and essential for the South's radio programmers and promotional insiders. This group of music trendsetters were oftentimes referred to as The Southern Mafia.

As the story goes, weeks earlier, during one of those heavy-drinking evenings, Tookie and Jimmy got into an altercation which spilled out into the driveway. Jimmy landed a right hook that left Tookie with a shiner. Tookie, recognizing Jimmy's importance, didn't hit back. Cooler heads prevailed, and the next day, Jimmy apologized like a true Southern gentleman. He told Frank, "I owe you one."

Well, Tookie wasn't one to forget a favor. Though, by then, the black tint under his eye had all but disappeared. He got on a plane back to Atlanta, called in the debt, and by the next week, a group of influential Southern radio stations had reported *'Take Me Home, Country Roads'* as a hot new single. From there, the RCA field staff took the song the rest of the way home to the top of the charts. The John Denver hit-making journey had officially begun. Frank "Tookie" Dileo literally took one for The Gipper—or in our case, The Nipper.

After *Poems, Prayers & Promises*, John spent considerable time recording follow-up albums at our RCA Studios. He'd often drop by just to chat or check his radio airplay and chart positions.

When he was recording, which was often, I'd swing down to the fourth floor to say hi to John and Milt. On one visit, John was on a break, juggling four softball-sized orbs.

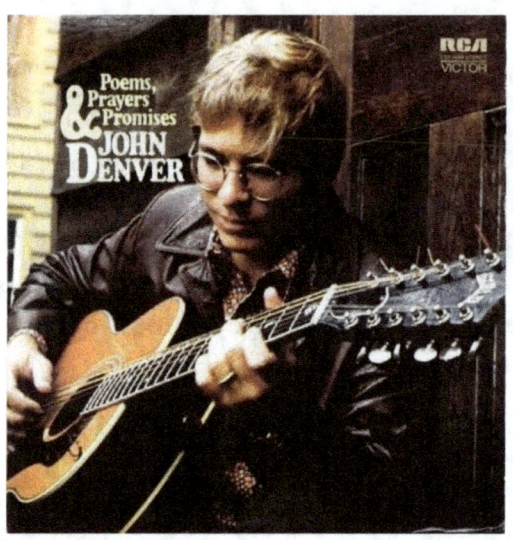

I was impressed and said, "Denver, you've got some major talent."

John replied, "You Wanta Try?" then grinned. "It's easy."

He then walked me through the basics—start with two in one hand, get a rhythm, then add the third. Within twenty minutes, I had three going. The juggling didn't last long, but long enough to feel like I accomplished something. I told him he was a good teacher. John laughed. "Not circus-ready just yet." And that, my friends, is my claim to fame, John Denver taught me how to juggle.

Over the years we got to know each other. I

learned he studied architecture in college. We were both fans of Buckminster Fuller and Frank Lloyd Wright. John was also ahead of his time with his concern for the environment, something he championed passionately. John was also a solid shortstop; he even played a few games with our Nipper Central Park softball team. When Michael Nesmith was in town, he played third base. John played shortstop. Tookie always insisted on pitching, and I rotated between center field and first base with Stu the Jew. Sometimes, members of The Guess Who joined in. Those friendly label-vs-label games were surprisingly effective for artist relations as well as bonding with promotional personnel from other record companies.

One day at the studio, we got into a conversation about names. I told him my birth certificate didn't say "Tom Cossie," but "Tom Surman." I wasn't Italian, my family was German and Polish. He laughed and said, "My birth name was Henry John Deutschendorf." He explained, "Henry John sounded too Greek, using two first names, and Deutschendorf wasn't exactly a radio-friendly name for an artist. I always loved Colorado—so John Denver it was."

After my ignominious departure from RCA, I continued to follow John's career, especially his television specials, most of them produced by Jerry Weintraub. By the 1980's and 90's, Jerry had become a major Hollywood mogul. Though Frank Mancini once told me, "If it wasn't for Jerry's wife,

Jane Morgan, no one would have known he existed." I later discovered Mancini's opinion was inaccurate.

When I first met Jerry Weintraub, he was quite dismissive. He was in Frank's corner office, and I was excited to come in and share my efforts with both my boss, Frank, and Denver's manager, Jerry Weintraub. I'd arranged phone interviews with stations across the country and was excited to share the news. Without letting me finish my pitch, Weintraub abruptly said, "not interested", and turned away to discuss other matters with Frank. I now knew how other staff members felt when Colonel Tom Parker visited RCA. I learned early on it didn't pay to be sensitive regarding unreceptive behavior from a manager.

A few days later, I saw John in the studio and shared the story about my brief meeting with his manager. I think I opened the conversation by saying, "Your manager is an asshole." I then explained how I had interviews set up and he just blew the whole thing off.

John told me, "That's just Jerry's personality. If you want better results try a different approach". He told me, "Instead of telling Jerry you had set up all the interviews, you should have posed it as a question and asked him, 'If I set up a series of ten or so radio interviews talking about the *'Poem's Prayers and Promises'* album, would you make John available?' For a long-haired country boy with granny glasses, John nailed the situation. He was right, it's often better to plant the idea, so it becomes their idea, and more than likely achieve the goal you wanted. Besides, Jerry liked to let people know who was in control and calling all the shots.

In an earlier chapter of this book, I mentioned some traits shared by highly successful managers. It seems that control is at the top of that list. Tony Defries with Bowie, The Colonel with Elvis, and Jerry with John Denver. As a 26-year-old Senior VP at a major record label, I initially found it challenging to yield some of my self-perceived importance and control over any situation. However, I came to understand the importance of recognizing who was paying the bills and funding the RCA operations. The profit from one multi-platinum album can cover a company's overhead for an entire year. When it comes to control, Money Talks, and when dealing with a manager of a major artist, stroking egos also has its benefits. John filled me in on a little history about Jerry Weintraub's background as manager of other recording artists before he married Jane Morgan. In Jerry's earlier days, he managed: Paul Anka, The Four Seasons, Jackson Browne, and Jimmy Buffett.

Reflecting on the past, both Mancini and Weintraub were part of the same social circle, were a decade older than me, and were involved in the New York City media industry. It is possible that Frank's dismissive remarks about Jerry's ascent to fame stemmed from his envy over Jerry's relationship with Jane Morgan. However, Weintraub's credentials as a manager are indisputable, having promoted tours for notable artists such as Sinatra, Elvis, Neil Diamond, and even Led Zeppelin. During the 1980's and 1990's, Weintraub also managed tours for The Four Seasons, Jackson Browne, and Jimmy Buffett. His accomplishments extend beyond music promotion to include film production credits for *Ocean's Eleven* and The Karate Kid series. Weintraub's extensive network of media contacts facilitated numerous television specials featuring John in subsequent years.

In October 1997, I received the unfortunate news that John had perished in a plane crash. Despite his expertise as a pilot, the small experimental aircraft he was operating lacked adequate gliding capabilities. Although it was reported there were no traces of drugs or alcohol in his system, I have always wondered whether he might have, lit up a doobie and neglected to check the fuel level before takeoff and subsequently ran out of fuel. John remained free-spirited until the very end.

It is notable to reflect on his final moments as he descended over the Pacific Ocean for what would be the most significant flight in his life, possibly saying his characteristic expression:

"Far out," one last time.

Chapter Eighteen

Politics of Dancing

Politics, whether in music or manufacturing, finance or film, infiltrate into every workplace. They creep in like background noise, quietly influencing every interaction, decision, and career trajectory. The music business, with the lure of fame, draws many into its orbit. In fact, as it turns out, the record industry is one of the most politically charged of all industries.

Most people don't enter the music industry because they crave a desk job or aspire to corporate maneuvering. They get involved because they love music. Pure and simple. Though once inside, they quickly discover that the climb to the top is less about music and more about mastering the maze of personalities, power structures, and politics that govern every step of the journey.

Take the 1960's and 70's, for instance. If you were a musician chasing that elusive pot of gold at the end of the rainbow, your first goal was to get signed. But before you ever cut a record, you had to navigate a corporate gauntlet. Your fate lay in the hands of the A&R director. The gatekeeper who decided whether your sound deserved a shot at immortality on vinyl. Once they cracked open the door, the real struggle would begin: branding, schmoozing, politicking. Even if you landed that coveted contract responsible for your success, you were suddenly one of dozens of artists vying for the same limited spotlight directed by the same people in promotion and sales.

This pattern isn't unique to music. In any business, anywhere people work together, there's a dance of control. You either hold the reins, or you're caught in someone else's harness. The emotional arc is predictable: you start with passion, hit the wall of politics, and either adapt, do drugs, or burn out, or a combination of all three.

At RCA Records, the corporate hierarchy mirrored most large companies. At the top sat the president, followed by Senior Vice Presidents overseeing A&R, promotion, press, marketing, and sales. When I moved to New York to work at RCA, all promotion reported to the Senior Vice President of sales. That structure flipped when my new boss, Frank Mancini, took the reins as Senior VP of Promotion with one condition; he, as Vice President of Promotion, would report directly to the president. His logic was sound. After all, you must create demand before you can convert interest into sales. But this triggered an age-old turf war. Sales blamed promotion when airplay subsided, and promotion blamed sales because records did not get into the stores quick enough to support the airplay. In the early 70's, Frank "Tookie" Dileo and I relocated to New York City; Tookie as National Director of Singles, and me as National Director of Albums. We immediately sensed the tension between the two departments. But we didn't let any reporting structure slow us down. As long as we had the freedom to do our jobs without the drama, we would be good.

During our time at RCA up to 1975, we had a great run delivering hit records with chart topping success. There were weeks when John Denver, Harry Nilsson, Jerry Reed, Dolly Parton, Jose Feliciano, The Guess Who, Main Ingredient, and a host of others of our artists, including Elvis, would all simultaneously be on Billboards charts. I must say Elvis, out of all the artists we promoted, probably required the least amount of work. Elvis was an institution at RCA Records. In comparison, I'm sure The Beatles shared similar status at Capitol Records. When an artist achieves that extreme level of success, the problem for promotion people was not trying to get airplay on radio, but which song or selection off an album should get the attention of radio. If every station was playing a different track and not focusing on one song, it became difficult to maximize chart impact. Which, in the long run, hurt sales and chart longevity.

In 1974, Frank Mancini stepped down for health reasons and I became RCA's Senior Vice President of Promotion at age 26. Tookie went over to Bell Records then went back to Pittsburgh to retire from the record business, run numbers and take sports bets. Some years later, Tookie, would be called back to Epic Records as head of promotion. Epic was a division of Columbia Records.

By the end of 1974, the new president of RCA decided that all promotional departments should go back to reporting to sales. This was not the only factor regarding Tookie and I leaving RCA, however, times were changing, and politics did play a role. As a Senior VP, the only commonality I shared with our new president, Ken Glancy, was an occasional sip of Dalwhinnie Highland Single Malt Scotch Whisky or a puff of a Cohiba cigar in the RCA executive dining room. When Mancini stepped down, his sales counterpart, Jack Kiernan, stepped in. He now had his wish to have both sales and promotion reporting to sales. That included myself and my 73 national and local staff team members. Jack, however, was cool and tried to make the merger work. He organized joint fishing and clam gathering trips on Long Island's South Shore. These events always helped in pulling both the sales and promotion teams together.

The transition was, at first blush, hard to handle, but Jack's new combined unit consisted of many of my former promotional people and the change melded together quickly. Around the same time as the department's merger, a series of drug related stories, involving the record industry, were once again topical in the news cycles. Those drug related headlines often appeared when there was a slow news cycle. To that end, one story would become my swan song. It took place at a radio station in Dallas.

My Southwest regional promotion man, Stewart, reportedly was accused of giving cocaine to a local station's music director. This incident was conveyed to a local Dallas TV station's news department by a promotion man who worked for Warner Brothers Records. Word got back to Jack from both his Dallas sales rep and from NBC's corporate office. (The station that aired the story also happened to be an NBC affiliate in Dallas.) I learned about the allegations of Stewart providing cocaine only moments before Jack called me into his office.

It was late in the afternoon, Jack said "Cossie, I received word from corporate that one of your promotion people gave drugs to a radio station in Dallas. You must fire him immediately before this shit gains traction."

At first, I thought, 'What's the big deal? If every promotional person I knew were to be fired for giving weed or cocaine to a radio station, there would be no one left in the business.'

Jack was concerned about corporate headquarters protecting their image due to NBC's government contracts, global broadcasting, and media licenses. I also knew the person who reported Stewart and doubted the credibility of the claim.

Jack said, "I mean now, fire him now".

I informed Jack that I would not terminate Stewart's employment until I had a conversation with him. Later that evening, Stewart shared his account with me, revealing the truth and the tension between him and his accuser. Despite my commitment to supporting my team, the allegations were substantiated, and given the broader implications for NBC, this posed a significant issue. Consequently, I understood the necessity of firing Stewart, even though I was dissatisfied with the origins and jealous motives of the person making the claim.

At 9:00 a.m. the next morning, I walked into Jack's office and saw a bottle of Jack Daniels and two glasses on his desk. Jack said, "Cos, you have two choices: resign or be fired. The Corporate office prefers firing because it's cleaner for them." After two drinks, I told Jack, "You will have my resignation on your desk within the hour."

RCA had provided excellent opportunities for me over the years, and I made sure my departure was as seamless and non-confrontational as possible. They let me resign gracefully, and in return, my exit was respectful of my former company. My positive approach to understanding the company's circumstances and my graceful exit would help me maintain an open avenue for future collaborations with RCA and their soon to be new owners, BMG.

Change can be either a bittersweet reflection on the past or an exciting opportunity to explore new territories. Often, change is triggered by external circumstances, yet we ultimately become our own architects of its outcome. When I said goodbye to my RCA staff, I was initially upset but then reflected on an amazing six year run I had with the company. Over the years, I had built strong relationships with the record industry trade magazines. They quickly noticed my departure and sought my perspective. I had nothing but positive comments about RCA and stated that it was time to pursue my ultimate dream of starting my own record label.

Chapter Nineteen

River Records - Saturn

Records Record Logic and

Companies

Most people carry fond memories of their hometowns, I'm no exception. My career in the music business had started in Pittsburgh, and since I had never relocated my family to New York, returning to Pittsburgh was a seamless transition. We still owned a small but comfortable home in the suburbs, and my wife and kids were well-acclimated to the Pittsburgh lifestyle. Plus, we couldn't have been in a better city for sports; the Steelers, Pirates, and Penguins were all thriving. Pittsburgh has always been a hidden gem for talent, across both sports and entertainment.

Speaking of sports, the city's legacy for producing great quarterbacks is unparalleled: Joe Namath, Jim Kelly, Dan Marino, Joe Montana, Johnny Unitas, and George Blanda — all grew up within a short drive from downtown. On the music side of talent, Pittsburgh was equally impressive, spawning recording artists like: Henry Mancini, Perry Como, Dean Martin, Billy Eckstein, Jimmy

Beaumont and the Skyliners, Phyllis Hyman, Donnie Iris (of The Jaggerz), The Vogues, Lou Christy, The Del Vikings, Frank Czuri (of The Silencers), Diamond Rio, Pure Gold, Norman Nardini, Joe Grushecky and The Iron City Houserockers, Pete Hewlett, T. Doverspike, James Blazer (of X15), Jim "Sputzy" Sparacino, Christina Aguilera, and jazz legends like George Benson, Stanley Turrentine, and Ahmad Jamal. On the progressive side of the artist spectrum, Andy Warhol grew up in the small Pittsburgh suburb of McKeesport, before making his way to fame in New York City.

It would be nice to say all this success came from the fresh air, but back in the 50's and 60's, with the steel mills in full swing, you'd pray for wind and rain just to share a breath of fresh air. (And for historical accuracy, I should note Christina Aguilera wasn't part of that original wave, her parents were more than likely kids themselves at the time.)

The year was 1976, the Bicentennial of the United States, and it also marked the launch of my ambitious new label, River Records. River Records would go down in history, not for hit records, but for having the most extravagant stationery ever created. I spent more on chrome-embossed six-color business cards, letterhead, and envelopes than I did on my entire first recording budget!

It was a rookie mistake, believing flashy

stationery would make the company. Throughout my life, I had a knack for doing things a little over the top, and this was no exception. The chrome embossing process cost ten times the price of normal stationery, and to "save money," I ordered 10,000 units to get a lower price per piece. Brilliant, right? I hadn't considered the possibility of failure. If River Records folded, I'd be stuck with truckloads of unusable, environmentally toxic paper. As it turns out, the stationery was the only hit to come out of River Records.

The music? Well, the records and groups I produced that year all ended up being picked up by other labels. For instance, I signed Diamond Reo to Doug Morris and Dick Vanderbilt's New York City based label, Big Tree Records. Our Pittsburgh demo tapes were strong enough to land us an album deal. In signing the band, Doug mentioned he had a good friend, Albert Grossman, who owned the state-of-the-art Bearsville Sound Studios in Woodstock, New York. If we were interested, he said, we could record there and even stay at Albert's residence while he was out of the country.

It was an incredible offer. Bearsville was the home studio to the legendary artists: Todd Rundgren, Meat Loaf, Foghat, The Dave Matthews Band, and The Isley Brothers.

And here we were, an unknown Pittsburgh band receiving red carpet treatment. I knew Doug and Dick from my earlier promotion days, and having a good, respectful relationship made it easier to secure this amazing opportunity.

The Bearsville residence itself was rustic yet luxurious, filled with Albert's eclectic artwork and upscale amenities. We spent a week recording before the band returned to Pittsburgh. A few days later, I received a call from Doug Morris. As I began thanking him, he interrupted me, not angry, just matter of fact. Albert had returned to Woodstock and discovered that several small paintings were missing. Since our band had been the only guests, it was implied, gently, but firmly, that we were responsible. To say I was embarrassed would be an understatement, I apologized and promised to investigate. The missing art was returned shortly thereafter, followed by two grueling weeks of heartfelt apologies. This incident was not only embarrassing but left a stain.

Bubs McKeg, Frank Czuri, Robb Johns, Norman Nardini

The next Diamond Reo album was not on Big Tree Records. Although we managed to chart a Top 50 Billboard single on Big Tree entitled "Ain't That Peculiar". I did give the band another shot at the plate. We recorded the next album "Dirty Diamonds" on Kama Sutra Records distributed by Buddah Records.

I'd love to chalk the theft up to sheer stupidity, but the truth is, the volatile cocktail of drugs and alcohol tends to summon demons that were never invited. Nearly every band I worked with eventually fell into the same traps; talent tangled up with self-destruction.

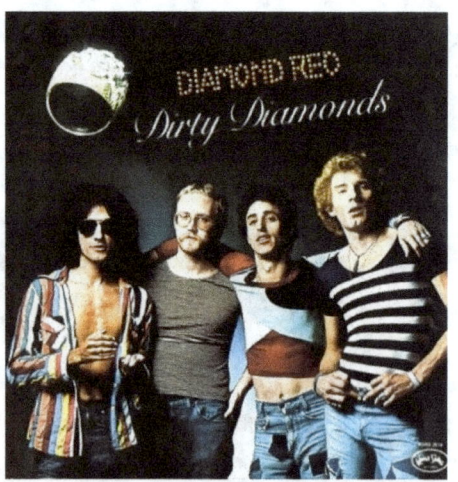

Frank Czuri, Warren King, Norm Nardini, Rob Johns

Some years earlier while I was working at RCA, I signed a Pittsburgh band named Sweet Lightning to an album deal at RCA. The lead singer, Pete Hewlett, had a great voice and some years later went on a worldwide tour as a harmonizing background singer with Billy Joel. This story is not about Pete but about his drummer and a disappearing drum set. Sweet Lightning was recording an album in Studio D, just six floors down from my RCA office in New York City. Buddy Rich, the legendary jazz drummer, had just wrapped up his session the day before, and his drums were still in the studio. Sweet Lighting's drummer couldn't resist testing them out. Days later after the band completed their tracks, the road crew packed up the bands equipment and headed back to Pittsburgh.

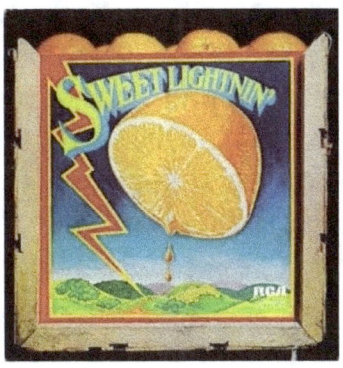

The following week, while attending a Sweet Lightning rehearsal, I spotted a drum kit on stage that didn't look familiar. After a closer look, I asked Bird, our band's drummer, when he bought the new drum kit. He casually said he'd had the drums for a while and then replied, "don't they sound amazing?" As I took a closer look at the bass drumhead, something looked strange. The large original letters "B R" were still highly visible in the upper corner of the drum face, and at the bottom of the drum face appeared to be the word "BAND" which was not so neatly whited out. The "B R" on the top left section of the head was turned into "BIRD" by using a black magic marker. The Buddy Rich, B R Band, drum set, had become the BIRD drum set.

I called Pete Spargo, a friend, and longtime engineer at RCA's Studio D, and apologized for the road crew's error. Pete laughed and said, "everyone on the fourth floor had been wondering where Buddy Rich's drum kit had gone, including Buddy." Thankfully, Pete agreed to keep things under wraps if I returned the gear immediately. I had the drums shipped back—minus the incriminating, altered "BIRD" drum face. Yet again, alcohol and amphetamines had fueled another stupid, and entirely avoidable mess.

These tales of poor judgment were especially disheartening because many of these bands were extremely gifted. But just as a major opportunity appears, they'd self-sabotage with an ill-timed act of immaturity or chaos. I often equate these situations in comparison to a young football player, who just got drafted with a promising career ahead, then screws up through some immature or stupid move, which usually involved drugs.

By 1979, my production and management company, Record Logic, had landed a multi-artist brand deal with Epic Records.

The roster included Graf, a band I signed out of Cleveland. I had Steve Katz, the guitar player for Blood Sweat and Tears, and brother of my attorney, Dennis Katz, to produce the album. Of all the bands I worked with from Cleveland, this band was the was one of the best. Frank Pellino on lead vocals and guitar, Jose Ortez on Drums, Peter Tokar on vocals and keyboards, and Tim Graziano, on bass guitar. The album was released on Precision Records distributed by CBS.

David Werner

We also signed David Kent, the keyboard player with the Hall & Oates band, and two artists from Pittsburgh, The Whizz Kid, David Werner, and The Silencers. Determined to produce the best recordings possible, I secured the top studios and talent. We recorded at Power Station in New York City, and I brought in Grammy-winning engineer and mixer Bob Clearmountain to produce both the David Werner and The Silencers albums.

David Werner's self-titled album, released in 1979, climbed into the top 60 on the *Billboard chart* Top 200. The Silencers' debut album, *Rock & Roll Enforcers*, produced and engineered by Bob Clearmountain, followed in 1980. I knew Bob was a star producer in the making, I'd seen him in action a year earlier while he engineered several hits for Chic at Power Station. He also did a great job producing the Silencers' album and even told me that if I brought the band back to New York for a live performance, he'd personally mix the show. That was huge. The band was hot, and now the best sound mixer in the city would be at the mixing board.

To capitalize on the momentum on the album and big budget video, I orchestrated a high-profile showcase for the album rollout at Trax, one of New York City's premier rock clubs. My goal was clear: impress the press, radio, industry trades, and Epic staff in one bold stroke.

Before the show, I laid down the law: *no drinking or drugs*. This was a pivotal moment, a professional milestone that required complete focus.

Bobby Clearmountain came in early for soundcheck and worked with the band. Everything sounded perfect. Afterward, the group returned to the hotel to rest and clean up around 3:00 p.m. The show time was set for 8:00.

Dennis Takos, Bird Foster,
Michael Pella, Frank Czuri, Warren King

I didn't anticipate the personal drama that was about to unfold. The band had brought wives and girlfriends to the city for this special performance. DT, the keyboardist, learned that his wife had invited her ex-boyfriend to the show. She dropped that bombshell right after the soundcheck and, also, that she was leaving DT. At that moment, whatever resolve the band had about staying sober dissolved instantly.

The band arrived at the club only moments before taking the stage. I could tell immediately something was off. Bobby leaned over during the first few songs and said, "The guys are wasted, especially DT. I think he's crying on stage." Sure enough, DT was visibly sobbing. At one point, he did a dramatic slide down his keyboard and kept going, right off the stage and falling behind one of the large speaker cabinets.

At first the crowd thought it was part of the act, until he didn't make it back on stage to finish the song.

The band tried to rally after a brief intermission and managed to limp through the rest of the set, closing better than they opened, but the damage was done. I later found out a fight had broken out at the hotel between the band's girlfriends and wives. A few fifths of bourbon and a lot of cocaine was consumed within hours before the show. Also, I was told DT's wife had not only left him, just hours before, but returned to the show with the boyfriend during the band's first song.

It was a long night for me and a short one for the audience, many of whom left midway through the show. One disastrous performance doesn't necessarily destroy a career. However, in this instance, it did not enhance my chances for the tour support I had anticipated from Epic. The band shooting themselves in the foot would be an understatement that evening. That afternoon and evening from 3:00 to 8:00 p.m., the band indulged in drama and substance abuse, ruining a crucial opportunity in their career.

Even my Electric Liturgy church band, The Mind Garage, was not immune to bad decisions. Their vice? Psychedelic drugs. Grass was commonly used, they never missed a gig and always performed dynamically on stage, but hallucinogens was one of their undoing's.

As the musical trends of the time dictated, I decided to rent a farm in the hills of West Virginia, just outside of Morgantown. In the mid 60's there was the group of amazing players called, The Band, who rehearsed and recorded a classic album, "Music from Big Pink", all developed in a country setting. As a result, every group felt it imperative to occupy a farm in the country, complete with a barn for inspiration and providing the environment and motivation to write hit songs. If I would have done my research back in 1968 about the recording of 'Music from Big Pink' I would have learned: 1. The music recorded from Big Pink was recorded at a studio in New York City. 2. Big Pink was a modest small three-bedroom home with pink aluminum siding on the outskirts of Woodstock and not a glamorous Pink Barn on a sprawling farm setting. 3. Not necessarily being inspired by the location, The Band's few songs that were inspirationally written at Big Pink could have been written anywhere. If this information had been available earlier, it would have been possible to avoid the costs associated with finding a farm as well as the incidents involving acid, gunshots, and conflicts with local residents.

The farm I rented consisted of 70 acres, featuring a large furnished farmhouse and two barns. The larger barn was converted into a rehearsal hall to accommodate the equipment and a P. A. system. Extra power was brought in to accommodate all the bands' amplifier stacks and cabinets. The believers in the Big Pink myth would have been impressed.

We were weeks away from recording, so I asked my Pittsburgh attorney and dear friend, Chris Copetas, to ride down with me to Morgantown. It was an early Saturday morning, and I wanted to remind the band we had a recording deadline and to check on their progress. To reach the farmhouse we had to drive up a two-mile dirt road which ran through the center of the property. Half the way up the road we heard loud and distorted feedback off in the distance, which seemed to be coming from the direction of the barn. Chris and I were about a quarter mile away from the farmhouse which was set back about 100 feet off the dirt road. As we were heading toward the house we ran into Jack, the keyboard player, hurriedly pumping a bike down the road toward us. We stopped the car and asked where he was heading. He said, "Away from the house". He looked a little distraught, so I asked him what was going on. Jack replied, "Since the house was shot up last night, everyone has scattered. I don't know where Ted and Norris went, and the last time I saw Larry, he was hiding out in a tree and howling at something down in the lower field. You can hear John, he's been playing for hours in the barn, and it sounds like his amps are turned up to 10!"

I said, "Ok, first, who was shooting up the house, and did anyone get hurt?"

Jack responded, "We all went into town last night, hit a few bars and picked up a few girls and brought them back to the house. and everyone was tripping and having a good time. Everything was ok until a few locals, in a car and pickup truck, kept cruising back and forth in front of the house. At first, they were just blowing their horns, then a few shots were fired at the house and the girl's names were called out. The girls ran out, and a few more shots were fired. Everyone in the band scattered. I haven't been back to the house since, so I don't' know anything else."

As Chris and I looked at each other, a bit speechless, I paused before asking him:

"So... do you still want to be my attorney?"

Months later, the second album was delivered to RCA and released. Unfortunately, the farm magic captured in "Music from Big Pink" was not to be found. And the group members went their separate ways.

Over the years, another label of mine, Saturn Records, produced over fifty projects and worked with an assortment of talented artists. Some of which were signed to major record labels through the production and management company Record Logic. Artists such as: Michael Wycoff, David Werner, and The Main Ingredient. Others had releases with Precision Records, managed by my brother Chuck: X15, EXP Express, The Alter Boys, and the Silencers.

Prime Time Music was a label we used for our rock projects which included the artists: King Creole, Joe Stark and Modern Man. The artists and projects which we kept on the Saturn Label brand were, George Romero's film soundtrack album, *The Day of the Dead*, soul singers Floyd Beck and Sputzy Sparacino, The Klass, The Irish group Patty O Furniture, Tony Granito and the Philadelphia Acapella group, The Foundation.

Returning to Pittsburgh after working at RCA allowed me to establish Street Stuff Music Inc., which encompasses publishing companies (Cosmosis Music- an ASCAP affiliate, Street Stuff Music – a BMI affiliate, and Cactus Music – an ASCAP Affiliate). We also established production companies, Record Logic and MK Productions.

Frank "Tookie" Dileo, my friend and promotion partner from our RCA days, also moved back to Pittsburgh, and did quite well for himself. That is, in addition to being the best bookie in the Burgh. Tookie would become Michael Jackson's manager, and responsible for the success of Michael Jackson's *Thriller* Album. Tookie also became a film star playing the role of Tuddy, in John Scorsese movie, *Goodfellas,* and played Mr. Big, in the *Wayne's World movie.*

During the editing of "Goodfellas," I was informed that Frank made acting seem effortless. Frank had recently purchased a ranch in Ojai, a flourishing film star community north of Los Angeles, Frank named his 30-acre estate

"The Tookarosa," inspired by his favorite TV show, "The Ponderosa."

Courtesy of Warner Brothers Films.
Caption: " Joe-You should have bought the Jeep. "

While visiting Frank, he gave me a tour of his ranch and invited me to stay for a while because two of the film's main actors, Ray Liotta and Joe Pesci, were coming by to purchase a jeep that Frank was selling to Joe. When they arrived, we gathered around the kitchen table. At one point, as Frank left the room, I asked Ray how it was working with someone like Frank, who had never taken an acting class. Liotta responded that Frank was on the money; whenever it was time for him to come on set, a crew member would call his trailer and Frank would deliver his lines in one take and then return to the trailer. According to Liotta, Frank was natural. I could only imagine that Frank's previous experiences as a booky, managing bets and collections, had served him well in preparing him for his new acting career, especially for his role in Goodfellas.

The year after moving back from New York City we threw a business party to celebrate our country's 1976 Bicentennial and a welcome back Tookie and Cossie picnic. We invited concert promoters, key radio personalities, retail store managers and entertainment industry friends. Jack Forsythe from the Pittsburgh Top 40 powerhouse 13Q Radio, brought with him the band Foghat, who played the day before at Three Rivers Stadium. Squiggy from TV show Laverne and Shirley was the home plate umpire for the Foghat concert, and he also attended the picnic.

This turned out to be one of many iconic Pittsburgh Picnics. Tookie and I did the cooking; I mean I did the grill work and Tookie did most of the eating. He did, however, earn the copious amounts of food eaten by pitching for both sides during our All-Star softball game in our back yard ballfield. As a Pittsburgh tradition, everyone was invited to bring a plate of their choice. Fog Hat and Squiggy didn't get the memo, however Bobby Z brought dozens of his famous Alice B. Toklas herb laced brownies. I remember my mom sitting in the kitchen playing backgammon with Harvey Camble, the owner of Mobile Records One Stop. She saw the brownies and proceeded to eat two of them, her backgammon game improved. After winning several games in a row, and not knowing the contents in those brownies she kept saying, "Those were the best brownies I've ever had."

Softball with the band Foghat

Tookie was always the pitcher, at picnics and
on the mound for RCA Nipper's softball

Cossie cooking and setting the woods on fire

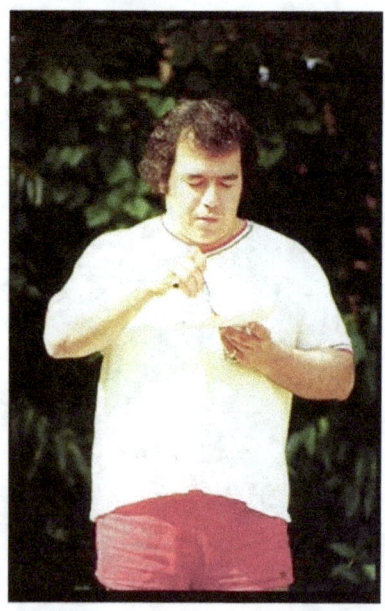

Tookie was also always on a diet

We also had a designated smoking area in the woods behind the house. To ensure no one got lost, Leo of the North, Pittsburgh's premier independent promotion man, directed picnic participants into the woods with a sign reading 'HOUH', our password for marijuana.

Leo of the North directing traffic into the woods

The Flying Zookhini's - Without the safety net

…and the crowd roared

The Picnics entertainment schedule included a backgammon tournament, an open bar, burgers and dogs by grill master Cossie, a trip to 'Houh' Woods, a softball game, and a performance by the amazing Flying Zookini's.

We would save the Zooks driveway performance until after everyone made a few trips into 'Houh' Woods. Those talented low wire and sometimes without the net performers, The Flying Zooks, did have real jobs as the camera and production crew from Pittsburgh's TV Channel 13, the local Public Broadcasting Station. In addition to their TV production skills, they were all wanna-be actors who would travel and perform charity benefits for the TV station. I guess not all of the Zooks were wanna-be actors. One Zook most certainly did make it. Film star, Michael

Keaton, of *Bat Man, Johnnie Dangerously, Mr. Mom, and Beetlejuice* did make his mark in film history. Michaels's name back in Pittsburgh at PBS was Michael Douglas. Since there was already a well-known Michael Douglas, he decided to become Michael Keaton.

Some of the picnic goers, fans and neighbors

Buzz Brindle, Zak, Jack and Romey Forsythe, Bobby Zurick, Jay and Marsha Brooks, and Jay Davis, look on in awe of the Flying Zooks performance

(All Photos of Fourth of July picnic
by Michael Valentine Smith)

Those who survived the day's picnic activities and made it into the night, had the opportunity to watch our double feature on a large screen outdoor TV. This Bicentennial Picnic's double feature was *Blazing Saddles*, and my favorite, Monty Python's, *Holy Grail*. For some reason the picnic and party gods of Pittsburgh would always keep us in their favor. Over the next forty years of

traditional 4th of July Picnics and Good Friday wine bottling events, no serious accidents ever occurred, and no fights ever broke out. Then again how many fights did you ever witness when people were smoking HOUH? Hey man chill, far out!

Chapter Twenty

The Story at Buddah Records

Atlantic Records and Chic

Midway through the Bi-Centennial year I came to realize the complexities of launching and building a company from the ground up. When you work as an employee with a nice salary and benefits you don't often appreciate the responsibilities and demands of ownership. Ownership means you have to make payroll, pay for all overhead, the cost of goods, all before taking your product to market. I hit that wall in 1976. A friend of mine, Ed Goodgold, was associated with various artists who recorded with Buddah Records, including Sha Na Na and the Monty Python Players, the esteemed English comedy group famed for 'The Holy Grail' and 'The Life of Brian'. I met Ed during my tenure at RCA, and he was aware of my experience working with a diverse array of artists. Buddah Records, though a much smaller company, had a similar diversified roster. Ed believed Buddah presented an ideal match for my promotion expertise. He set up a meeting with Art Kass.

Buddah and Kama Sutra Records were New York City based labels, initially distributed by

MGM in the mid-sixties. At first these two labels were famous and synonymous with a form of music called bubble gum music. Lighthearted pop music featuring the 1910 Fruit Gum Company, Melanie, The Ohio Express, The Loving Spoonful, and The Lemon Pipers who had a hit with their song, *'Green Tambourine'*. Art Kass, the Buddah/Kama Sutra president, cut ties with MGM in 1969. He then brought in sales and promotion guru Neil Bogart to run Buddah and all the subsidiary labels between 1969 to the end of 1974. Neil and Art had a long string of hit single records, which included: *'Oh Happy Day'* by the Edwin Hawkins Singers, The Five Stairsteps *'Ooh Child'*, *'The Rapper'* by the Jaggerz, The Stories *'Brother Louie'* and hits by Gladys Knight and the Pips, *'Midnight Train to Georgia'*, and *'You're the Best Thing That Ever Happened to Me'*.

After a five-year run at Buddah, Neil left the company and moved to California to found Casablanca Records. In 1976 a large investment company, who was funding Buddah, declared bankruptcy. Art Kass pooled all his resources in an attempt to reclaim his company. It was at this time he called on me to run all record promotional operations. Art concentrated most of his resources and efforts on developing a film called *Pipe Dreams*, produced by Gladys Knight and her husband. Between 1976 and 1977, we achieved notable chart success with Norman Connors through the single *'You Are My Starship'*, featuring vocals by Michael Henderson and

Phyllis Hyman. The track reached Number One on the Jazz charts and peaked at Number Five on the R&B charts. Norman Connors, an esteemed jazz drummer, also served as the producer for this record.

We also had a top five pop and number one disco hit, entitled 'More More More', sung by Porno star turned recording artist Andrea True. As I mentioned our roster was diversified. During this era at Buddah, the policy for bringing new product to the label seemed to be, if you had a good sounding record and you could deliver it to the company with little to no cost, Buddah would press, release, promote and market the record. In return, you would receive a larger share of the royalties should the record sell. Greg Diamond, Andrea True's producer and co-writer of 'More More More', made that deal.

Artists such as Phyllis Hyman, the Tramps, Melba Moore, and Michael Henderson had previously achieved commercial success with Buddah and secured their contracts earlier. These artists had finished records prepared for release, having established agreements before the introduction of the new hybrid artist contract signing program.

The majority of releases at Buddah during this period were R&B records, except for The Charlie Daniels Band, who had experienced prior chart success. Art, at this time, was strapped for cash. He needed an influx of funds to continue to operate. He decided to sell Charlie's contract to

CBS to raise the funds to keep Buddah's doors open.

During the summer of '77 I planned a trip with our National R&B Promotion Director extraordinaire, Alan Lott, to attend the Black Music Seminar in LA. This was a convention geared specifically to R&B radio, retail stores, and record company promotional executives to gather, exchange ideas, and attend meetings. Mainly, these events were for socializing with colleagues over food and drinks. Our group of record business professionals loved those conventions that often became elaborate parties, but essential work still got done.

I remember this trip well. Art gave me a postdated check for 3 grand, made out to cash for walking around money during the convention. Both of Alan's and my travel expenses went on my American Express Card and the hotel was covered by the company. When I arrived in LA, my first task was to find someone who had the appropriate amount of cash and would be willing to hold the check for a week or until funds were available to cover the check.

Ray Anderson, my former RCA regional promotion manager, met Alan and I at LAX and we drove to the Bonaventure Hotel. I told Ray what I needed to do regarding a postdated check and asked him if he knew anyone who would be willing to do me a big favor. I needed someone who would be cool about the favor because, back then, when someone did a major favor for you, you knew you would be asked, at some point, to return that favor. Ray thought for a minute then said. "There is a spinner I know who plays records at a club where I hang out in Marina Del Ray. This kid was the first in LA to play your Andrea True single. He knows who you are from our days working together at RCA. He will be at the convention tonight, and I'll set up a meeting." The spinner who Ray referred to was Marc Kreiner, local record promoter and highly popular LA club Disco DJ.

That evening we were standing outside of the hotel when a yellow Porche pulls up in front, with the vanity license plate reading '3 Dog NT'. A tall Hollywood looking guy, long blondish hair and mustache, jumps out, leaving the car running and comes up and gives Ray a hug, turns to me and says, "Tom Cossie, nice to meet you, and no problem with the check, Ray told me everything."

I immediately thought to myself, what did Ray tell this guy. I refocused and reflected, 'if only everything in life could be this easy'. Marc was a tall kid who appeared to be in his early twenties. He was dressed in a festive Hawaiian shirt, Calvin Klein Jeans, and wore engineer boots that had to increase his height by two inches, which made him at least 6'6". I refer to Marc as a kid, as I'd just turned an old thirty years of age, and to me, everybody was a kid. It was apparent Marc had been at this hotel many times before, the valet brought his keys back to him while we were having drinks at the bar.

It seemed to me Marc Kreiner had his shit together, his social skills in order, was cocky enough to get things done, and crazy enough to cash a postdated check.

The next morning Marc and I drove over to Sherman Oaks to a bank where he kept a safe deposit box. He explained, he usually didn't carry around three grand in his back pocket, so the trip was necessary. Driving around with Marc in the valley was an experience in itself. Girls pulled up, honking their car horns, giving thumbs up and shouting, "Yeah! Three Dog Night." Marc honked back, smiled, and waved. This passion play repeated several times on our way to the bank before I caught on to what was happening. Marc had the LA scene down to a science. Marc did look like one of the singers in Three Dog Night, and that, along with the vanity license plate, and Porche. Well, people want to meet celebrities and Marc played the part well. I tuned to Marc and said, "Amazing...Only in Hollywood. "

We arrived at the bank. In goes Marc and moments later out he struts, jumps in the car and hands me a white envelope containing some 50's but mostly 100-dollar bills. He said, "I assumed you wanted large bills." I said yes, then told him I would personally guarantee the check and knew I owed him one.

Marc said "I know you're good for it, you have good friends here in LA."

The R&B Conventions were by far the most fun of all industry conventions. Those events were three days of hanging by the pool, drinking, and running around to see all the various companies' artists, who just so happened to be playing at all the most popular local venues. Record labels in LA took advantage of having a captive audience of radio programmers from around the country in their hometown for three nights during the convention. When you have a new artist with a new release, and those artists just so happen to be playing in town when the industry makes an appearance, well, do you think that's a coincidence? It was a win for everyone. The club owners sold the evening to the highest record company bidder, the fans got to see the hottest new recoding stars in an intimate club setting and the artist loved the close up and personal club setting to perform in front of radio programmers from around the country.

I didn't want to miss seeing my old friend from WAMO in Pittsburgh, Brother Matt, or Franky Crocker from WBLS in New York and a few friends from Chicago radio. All the one-on-one meetings were arranged. I hoped to run into Butter Ball, Philadelphia's WDAS music director, Joe "Butter Ball" Tamburro. Butter was special. and Alan had to set up, what he called, "A stop on The Butter Ball tour." If you wished to meet with Butter, you had to reserve a spot on the 'tour'.

Each year, you would have to log onto his daily restaurant tour, 'The Butter Ball Food Tour'. It was the only way to spend time with 'Butter'.

Tom Cossie and Brother Matt

His assistant would pencil you in for a visit during one of two breakfasts, one of three lunches or one of two dinners during each day of his stay. There was also a rumor of a few snack stops between the big three meal destinations. I don't know how much he ate at each of those snack meeting layovers, but he always ate well during our scheduled dinner restaurant visits. It was always great to see "Butter", He knew the music, had a great sense of humor and always treated everyone with a loving respect.

On my first trip to Philly as the regional promotion man at RCA, I met 'Butter' and his Program Director, Jimmy Bishop. At the time I thought it unusual that a white Italian boy named Tamburro, would be the Music Director at the number one black radio station in Philadelphia. Though over the years, I worked with mostly black radio stations across the country. It seemed most of those R&B station's personnel were color blind when it came to our industry. I guess I shouldn't have found it unusual in my world as it related to R&B Music. Most of the hit records I've been associated with were by predominately black artists. I always felt comfortable in the black community. So much so I would end up being the co-publisher of the R&B Report in 1988.

Back to the R&B Convention in LA. It was the last day of Sidney Miller's Black Radio Convention. My business was transacted and to show my appreciation to Marc Kreiner for his trusting support, I asked him if he wanted to take a trip to Palm Springs with Ray Anderson, me, and two of Rays music programmer friends.

Ray had a good friend at one of the upscale hotels in Palm Springs and were given a better than family rate deal on four rooms. Our business meetings in LA were complete and since I still had some money in my pocket, I decided to go big and rent a Rolls Royce from Budget in Beverly Hills. I loved the 70's. You could rent any high-end car you wanted at the upscale Budget Rental location in Beverly Hills for $175.00 a day plus milage. The thought of motoring around Greater L.A. in a Rolls for a few days, was kind of sweet. We had three cars making the trip. I rented this beautiful burgundy Silver Cloud. This particular one was unique as all the other Rolls they had on the lot were black.

Marc and I drove together to Palm Springs, allowing us plenty of time to become better acquainted. He had a strong desire to get into the music business in a major way. I remember telling him how much I appreciated his trust regarding the cash and check situation, which he acted on without hesitation. He told me I had a good vibe and strong reputation for honoring my word.

When we checked into the hotel, I gave the Rolls key to the valet. I watched him write Burgundy Rolls on the ticket. Two hours later, Ray and his guests met Marc and I outside the hotel entrance and we decided to dine at Melvyn's, one of Frank Sinatra's favorite Palm Springs restaurants. I told the valet we had the burgundy Rolls. Moments later the car arrived, we got in and something seemed amiss. I thought I remembered the Rolls that we drove down was burgundy with black interior, not tan interior. Having just finished a few cocktails and polishing off a doobie, my comprehension wasn't crystal clear, but I still said to myself, 'Nah!' This has got to be our car, It's burgundy. How many burgundy Rolls can there be in this one parking lot?'

We drove to the restaurant, had a great dinner with three bottles of Dom Perignon. I ordered the first bottle and one of Ray's buddies ordered the next two. I never liked to order Dom at restaurants. For some reason it never bothered me to eat the 100% markup on a $30.00 bottle of nice wine, but 100% markup on a $175,00 bottle of Champaigne was a road too far.

I asked Ray's guest why he ordered a second and third bottle while only drinking one glass of champaign during the entire dinner. The reply was, "Because I can. And to be honest, I don't really like champaign that much anyway."

I didn't say anything but thought to myself what a bullshit and decadent spoiled brat attitude. I was picking up the check! The night was young, and so I suggested, "It's early, let's take a ride out into the desert." Whereupon we headed toward the Saltan Sea. Halfway there on the dark, desert highway, I had thoughts of returning with one less guest, however my, 'peace be with you', seminarian upbringing, as brief as it was, overruled my guttural emotions of wanting to strangle the guy. We all rolled the windows down, enjoyed the fresh desert air and shared a joint, before rolling back to the hotel.

The next morning, we decided to check out. I realized we had far exceeded my expenses after our dinner at Melvyn's. We could ill afford an additional evening in Palm Springs. As we checked out, I asked for the burgundy Rolls. Our car was brought around and the valet asked if by some chance we may have taken the wrong Rolls last night. I casually replied, "I don't think so, we took the Burgundy Rolls you gave us."

The valet told us "The couple who checked out earlier this morning, in their burgundy Rolls, complained about a heavy aroma of marijuana in their car and they blamed us for smoking grass in their vehicle."

Hmm, apparently more than one burgundy Rolls was possible.

The good news was we didn't do any damage, other than adding a few miles to that couple's Burgundy Rolls Royce with the tan interior. The additional good news was I also saved $125.00 not having to pay the extra dollar per mile when turning the car back into Budget Rental.

I flew back to New York, and on Monday met Art who was happy I worked things out during my trip. He told me the company was taking a turn for the worse, but he would make sure the check he gave me would be good. It was apparent he had extended himself well beyond his means.

A few weeks later, an old friend and composer from Philadelphia, Blood Hollins, stopped by my office at Buddah. He had just finished a session he was producing at Sigma Sound and told me he met three session musicians who were exceptional. They'd given him a demo tape they'd been shopping, looking for a record deal. He told me they'd been turned down by several record companies. I had to explain to him Buddah had a moratorium on signing any new artists until further notice as directed by the President, Art Kass.

Curiosity being part and parcel of the music business, I asked Blood what he knew about the tape. He said he used two of the guys, the rhythm guitar, and bass player, on sessions. They had a band in which he thought they were going to call Sheik, like SHEIK, but they spelled it CHIC. Their names were Nile and Bernard. They also had a smokin' drummer they worked with, Tony Thompson

I put the tape on and the first song on the demo was a song called *'Everybody Dance'*, which sounded great. The second one was titled, *'Dance, Dance, Dance'*. I listened twice to each song and said, "Blood, those demo's sound more like finished records. If I was at a different place, I would go to the wall to sign these guys."

He then told me, "They also write all of their own songs, including the ones we just heard."

That was music to my ears. These songs were well written, and the musicianship was outstanding, yet dynamically simple and memorable. The rhythm section, bass, drums, and rhythm guitar was like hearing one instrument. I asked Blood if he could leave me the tape. To which he replied, "That's why I brought it to you."

I went home that night and pondered, 'how can I get this project in the hands of our company'. I felt I had just listened to two hit records. Usually, people would bring you a tape of an artist or group. You'd listen to five or six songs and couldn't pick out any one song that you felt was remotely close to being a hit record. I even liked the band name but didn't know which Sheik or Chic direction in which they were going to take, the middle eastern Sheik, or the more elegant and classy use of the word Chic. The latter turned out to be the case.

The next morning, I played the tape for Art Kass. He said he agreed with my evaluation, but Buddah had no extra resources to either sign or make the records. Things were heading in the wrong direction when instead of getting a paycheck or reimbursement of expenses, you were offered the title of General Manager. Four of us were presented with that opportunity, everyone declined. Things were very tight at Buddah.

After I left Art's office, I was more depressed than ever. The next morning, I waited until noon, 9 am California time, then called my new best friend, Marc Kreiner. I told him I just heard what I felt was a number one record and if he wanted to get involved, I would bring him into the deal. Marc sounded interested, so I sent the tape by overnight mail.

Two days later he called, "You are on the money, both songs are great. They sure don't sound like demos. I know I can get these played just as they are. Especially *Dance, Dance, Dance (Yowsah, Yowsah, Yowsah)'*.

I explained to Marc, Buddah was in a transition. If he had the means to pay off the studio bill and secure the tapes from the studio, his money would be reimbursed, plus have a share in royalty ownership.

Our plan was simple, we would cut acetates and take it to key Disco DJ spinners and create a ground roots demand. (acetates were hard resin coated metal playable discs, masters used to produce the actual records). This was a process I had successfully done ten years earlier when I was spinning records at clubs in Pittsburgh. The process worked then, and I felt it would work now. There would be little or no risk to Buddah because if we got the DJ action, the demand would follow. Marc agreed but first Dennis and I had to figure out the money required to make this happen.

Nile Rodgers number was on the demo tape box so I called and asked if he and Bernard would be available to meet the next day. When we met, I told them their demo sounded better than most finished masters and I felt we could make it happen.

I was especially impressed with their belief in the development of their music. They had invested in themselves, gone into a top quality recording studio, brought in strings and, by the sound of the vocal tracks, added the best background singers in the city. All this with the amazing rhythm section of Nile Rodgers, Bernard Edwards, and Tony Thompson, made the perfect package. The only process left would be to master these songs, cut some acetates, and off we would go to the races.

The mastering process is when you take the final mixed tape into the mastering lab where the most intense listening takes place. The music is played over a wide variety of speakers, from car radio setups to large cabinet speakers, the kind you hear at dance clubs, as well as listening and comparing the sonics through various typical home stereo speakers. The purpose of this process is for the engineer to apply additional dynamics to the overall sound with compression and equalization. This process optimizes the overall sound of the record. Sounds like a lot of mumbo jumbo but when this fine tuning is done correctly, the recording will sound great no matter where you listen, at home, at the concert hall or in your car.

To make this Chic deal happen, we needed to pay the studio to have access to the recordings. The cost for the studio recordings was close to seven grand. I called Marc and reiterated that both Nile Rogers and Bernard Edwards were personally and creatively, the real deal. I felt these guys, along with their drummer, Tony Thompson, were the best rhythm section I'd heard since The Funk Brothers, the best recording studio musicians from the old Motown days. Those Detroit based session guys played on every Motown hit for over twenty years. Great players have the ability of making the complex sound simple. I felt we had the second coming with Chic.

Marc Kreiner was one of a kind. The next day he was on a plane, with a checkbook in hand, heading to New York City. He had family connections in New York and planned to stay at the Plaza Hotel. I called my old friend Dennis Katz, who worked with me as the head of A&R when we were both at RCA. When he left RCA,

Dennis went into private practice law representing musicians like Lou Graham, the lead singer of the band Foreigner, Angela Bowie, David's first wife, Lou Reed and several other notable celebrities. My first course of action was to have Dennis set up a company for Marc. My recommended name for Marc's company was MK Productions. Marc could then sign Chic to a production deal to purchase and represent the recording, then sign the rights over to Buddah, who would take over to manufacture, promote, market. and sell on a worldwide basis.

We met with Nile and Bernard the next day and made the deal. Chic was now signed to MK Productions. It was our unanimous decision that our first single should be *'Dance, Dance, Dance'*, the song in which Nile performed those three noteworthy words; using a megaphone sounding voice; *Yowsah, Yowsah, Yowsah.*

The next step was to bring the product to Buddah so we could release our first single. I negotiated with Buddah, on Marc's behalf. Art said he would have his business department prepare a contract. In the meantime, Marc and I decided to have about ten acetates made. Art told us to deliver the master tapes over to Frankford Wayne, the mastering lab he used for years on all Buddah product. Again, our reason for the advance discs of *'Dance, Dance, Dance'* was to create buzz with key disco spinner friends of Marc's in New York City, LA., and Boston.

The master tapes were now the property of MK Productions until the record deal was signed. Then all rights would be turned over to the record label for manufacturing, promotion, sales and distributions.

When Marc and I went over to pick up the acetates, the business office at Frankford Wayne said they wouldn't release anything until Buddah's bill was paid in full. It seemed that Buddah owed Frankford Wayne more than a year's worth of mastering, which totaled well over $75,000 dollars. Not good news for us, but we still had in our possession a backup copy of the master tapes. Nick, a contact of mine who worked at Frankford, quietly slid two acetates into my case. I now had a reference lacquer to the mastered tape. I thought any prolonged delay at this point would kill the project.

I decided to call Dennis King, who was an engineer and contact I knew at Atlantic's Records studios just off Columbus Circle. I brought to the Atlantic studio the safety master tape and one the Frankford Wayne acetates for reference. Dennis remastered and cut the 10 discs we needed. We distributed the acetates and within a week we generated airplay in the New York City, Boston, and LA dance clubs on 'Dance, Dance, Dance' became the talk of the industry. The dance crowd response to this record reminded me of years earlier when I played the song, Hanky Panky at my club dances. People would be cheering and singing along with the song. Everyone wanted to know what the *Yowsah Yowsah Yowsah* record was and where they could get a copy.

One of the key stops in laying the groundwork buzz on Chic was meeting with John Luongo, a notable remixer/DJ in Boston and New England market. Luongo also started the Boston Record Pool, one of the first three record pools in the United States. Record pools are subscription services that would provide DJs with access to a curated library of music tracks, often including exclusive edits, remixes, and other DJ-friendly versions.

We played the record for John, and he requested an acetate so he could make copies for all the DJs in the Boston and New England market. He also owned a magazine called Nightfall and was both a club jock and a radio DJ with significant influence.

John took the acetate to Boston and made tape copies for all the top DJs. They had the song well before it was ever released. He reported the song to the Billboard Club chart that he managed for the city of Boston. The next week the song came up on the charts as Number One and simply said *'Dance, Dance, Dance'* by Chic (Tape Copy)

When John called us and told us that the record had appeared at the top of the chart, that blew us away as we were negotiating with Atlantic at the time. That gave us extra clout to help close the Atlantic deal.

After completing this impressive work, Marc and I offered John the position to manage MK Dance and oversee all promotion and marketing for the company. This was essential because promoting and marketing dance music requires a strong team to coordinate all record activity to maximize chart success. In the years to come we would be proven right winning Billboards Dance Company of the year awards.

What took place then can only be described as remarkable. Jerry Greenberg, one of my promotion man idols from ten years ago when I worked at Hamburg Brothers, was now President of Atlantic Records. Jerry called and asked me to tell him the full story about this record and the group. He told me his promotion team in the NYC said our record was kickin' ass on the streets. Greenberg, being a former promotion man at heart, was always in pursuit of a hit record. He wanted this record to be on Atlantic. Marc had returned to LA earlier that week, I called him and explained that Atlantic wanted the single as well as to sign the group. Atlantic was also willing to have the group start working on the first album of a multi-album deal.

Personally, I was caught between a rock and a hard place. I still worked for Buddah, but did not have a contract with the label, and the company owed me over two months' worth of expenses. It was also apparent that Buddah did not have the financial ability to even have the record mastered or take any future steps to deliver this product. I'd made a commitment to Marc and couldn't let him hang in the wind.

During my conversation with Jerry, I told him my situation with Buddah, the money they owed me personally, as well as my commitment to Marc, who had invested a lot of time and money into the project. The next morning, I met Jerry at Atlantic Records with Dennis Katz, who brought with him a copy of the signed MK production contract between MK and Chic. Jerry looked the contract over and gave it to the Atlantic's attorney, Gary Baker. By the end of the day, Atlantic presented Dennis and I with their offer. Greenberg included the condition that I would either be part of or represent MK Productions going forward. If that was acceptable, they would pay me the money

Buddah owed me from back expenses, give MK Productions enough points to make Nile and Bernard happy, as well as enough points to make Marc happy. They would also give Art Kass a percentage of profit in the first album. The deal was generous, and extremely fair to all parties.

I asked Marc what he thought about the offer and without hesitation, he was on the next plane back to NYC and we both signed Chic to Atlantic Records. During the transitions between MK Productions, Buddah, and Atlantic, several tumultuous conversations did take place. However, money and business savvy on Atlantic's part, resolved all issues.

Tom Cossie, David Glew, Jerry Greenberg, Dennis Katz
Front row; Bernard Edwards and Nile Rodgers.
(Photo by: Bob Defrin)

Jerry Greenberg's executive decision making paid off big for Atlantic. Our first three Chic albums generated over $40 million dollars in revenue for Atlantic Records over three years. Starting in 1977, our first platinum album, Chic, featured hit singles: 'Dance, Dance, Dance' and 'Everybody Dance'. Oursecond album, C'est Chic, released in 1978 included Atlantic's best-selling single 'Le Freak', and 'I Want Your Love'. The third album, Risque, featured my personal favorite Chic song, 'Good Times', and the single 'My Forbidden Lover'.

The Canadian sales award, as shown on the plaque, was interesting because Canada like many other international markets have their own regulations regarding gold and platinum certification. In most cases the number of units is calculated to the country's population. For example, in Canada a gold record is 40,000 units and a platinum record is 80,000 units. To let you know how popular the song *'Le Freak'* really was, the Canadian Platinum Certification above states that this one single record sold over 450,000 units in Canada alone. That's a combination of both single 45 RPM records and the 12-inch extended mixed version of the single. Most countries combine both as singles since it's one song. The USA single sales of *'Le Freak'* sold over 6,000,000 copies

Producers Nile Rodgers and Bernard Edwards also wrote and produced for Atlantic the number one hit, *'We Are Family'* for the Atlantic artists Sister Sledge. The Chic journey continued up through the years to their last live performance in 1996. Nile and Bernard performed their final concert together, Live at Budokan, at the Budokan Arena in Tokyo. Shortly after that concert, Bernard passed away.

American Gold and Canadian Platinum Certification

If you were ever a fan of Chic, try to find a video copy of that Budokan performance. It was amazing. One view and you will see why Chic was considered the number one dance band of all time.

The Journey Continues

Welcome to The Plaza

Since none of us had an exclusive working arrangement between Chic and MK Productions, Marc, Nile, Bernard, and I worked separately on many independent projects, and Dennis Katz served as everyone's attorney. This was not an uncommon practice in the record industry. One well-known law firm, Grubman, Indursky, and Shindler, not only represented most of the major record company presidents and their contracted employees, but also represented the artists signed to those labels. Surprisingly not many conflicting lawsuits emanated out of what would appear to be collusion. I guess there was enough money going around that no one complained.

As previously mentioned, the late 1960s and early 1970s were significant periods in music. Marc and I expanded the MK brand by establishing a dance music company with locations in Beverly Hills and New York City. The New York division of dance music promotion was managed by Johnny "Bongo" Luongo, a DJ associate from Boston. With several chart successes, MK promotions represented numerous labels in the industry that produced dance music. The company's performance on the Billboard dance charts was notable.

In 1978, MK received the top nomination for Billboard Disco Company of the Year at an event held at the NYC Hilton Hotel. At that time, MK had recently achieved number one positions on the Dance, R&B, and Pop charts with 'Le Freak', and the next Chic release, 'Good Times', was forthcoming. To mark the occasion, Marc and I organized a party in New York City during Billboard's convention meetings and awards dinner.

Marc and I both loved the Plaza Hotel. We thought it would be cool to rent the top floor of the hotel for three days during that Billboard convention. I don't know if you are familiar with the Plaza Hotel on Fifth Avenue, but I always marveled when looking up to the top floor seeing all those large double door dormer windows under a gable roof facing Central Park. Very French Renaissance. I soon found out that those huge windows opened to a beautiful fresh air view of the park. Back then there must have been no government regulations regarding safety bars or window protection devices.

My theory was, the government believed if you could afford to rent this suite, why the hell would you want to jump?

A week before the dinner awards, Marc and I were given a tour of that entire 18th floor suite. As it turned out the entire floor was one large twent room, two floor suite designed for single occupancy. One suite, twenty rooms, complete with billiard room, two kitchens, parlor rooms, a large walk-in temperature-controlled wine vault, and bedroom mini suites with amazing views of Central Park. We said to each other, 'Why not? This looks like a good place to hold a party'.

One of the coolest features of this floor was it had its own elevator. An elevator that went only to one floor, the 18th floor. If you were using this elevator you had to know the key code to reach your destination. The elevator was located on the far side of the lobby directly across from the famous Plaza Oyster Bar. Its entrance was somewhat hidden around a corner, so the elevator location was not obvious.

Our invited guests kept getting lost. We finally had to post someone at the walkway in front of the Oyster Bar, keeping an eye out for people with that lost look in their eyes. The password was MK and our lookout had to enter the code in the elevator before it operated. It was a three-day party so we couldn't be too frivolous with our invites.

We had the feeling we were going to win the Billboard award so why not celebrate in style. Worst case scenario, we were coming off a major hit record, 'Le Freak', and Atlantic Records was about to release 'Good Times'.

We talked the hotel into giving us a special rate, this was years before trivago, so we cut our own deal and agreed to use the Plaza's hotel kitchen for all food, appetizers, alcohol with mixers and Champaigne, We were above board with ordering copious amounts of food, spirits and mixers, but when it came to the Champaigne, we were less above board.

Marc and I also owned a limousine company in New York City and in LA, called Fleetwood Limousine. This was a bi-costal business that was destined to lose money. All of our artists would use our limo services, we never thought to charge them, and the few times when we did, they didn't pay us anyway. Not exactly our best business model, but it did provide a great perk to the artists. Pete and Eddy were our main drivers and at this Plaza party they came in handy.

We priced out the Plaza champaign list and Dom Perigone was $275.00 a bottle, and Perrier Jouet wasn't that much less at $175.00. Well, we had to make it look good, so we ordered one case of Dom and one case of Perrier Jouet from room service. Then we had Pete and Eddy make a run over to Sherry Lehmann's, my favorite liquor store in the city, to buy ten more cases of each. Sneaking twenty cases of champaign up to the top floor, required some fancy footwork, however, Pete and Eddy were up to the task.

As an aside, I recently spoke with a dear friend of mine, Tommy Silverman, I told Tommy I was in the process of writing my first of several books and wanted him to know I had just returned from LA and ran into our old friend, Marc Kreiner, who I hadn't seen in over forty years. Tommy's reply was, "Those were the days, When I dropped out of graduate school where I was studying environmental earth science and geology. Scott Anderson was doing the R&B charts at Cashbox. I made my first business trip to LA (1978 summer). I then opened an office in an apartment I rented, where Marc, Scott, and I lived. We planned on publishing Disco News right from that apartment. Before we published our first issue, we went to the Disco forum at the NY Hilton and you guys had a party at the penthouse of the Plaza. You had cases of Dom Perignon and Perrier Jouet in the wine vault. I met Nile there. I met August Darnell there. We hung out until 4am, at least. I remember we snuck out on the roof and stole the Plaza flag, then took it up to Colby College in Maine where we all had lived in a fraternity together and run the radio station up there until 1976."

"You taught me what "abundance" means."

In the early 80's, Tommy went on to launch his own record label TommY BoY Records, and a line of clothing. His roster included Queen Latifah, Coolio, Naughty by Nature, House of Pain and The Force MD's. TommY BoY was one of the pioneers of Hip Hop music.

The Plaza party was a major success, and as predicted, we did win the Billboard Award. These party events were always productive. You merge hundreds of record people together: artists, managers, A&R people, attorneys, record executives, media magazines, and promoters all having a few drinks, there's good food, and all are in excellent spirits. This was neutral territory. No one was worried who was going to pick up the check for the food, drinks, and drugs. Everyone assumed we would and did most of the time.

Everyone was relaxed and no one was out to sell you anything, yet everyone had something to sell, and this environment was conducive. These events were an incubator for future business deals and by three or four in the morning, everyone was loose as a goose. Some of the best reasoned and thought-out business deals were contemplated and tentatively agreed on. That is, until the next day when no one could remember a thing as to what happened the night before.

Chapter Twenty One

Ocean Ariola

Marc Kreiner and I were on a roll! It was 1979 and by the end of the year the Disco and Dance music craze would have made its final surge in popularity. We had three multiplatinum Chic albums and a dance promotion company that was rockin'. We were also approached by two industry pioneers, Jay Lasker and Howard Stark, to start a new record label with their German based parent company, Ariola America. When you consider the image of a historic record executive, Jay Lasker would be that person. Jay was with Decca Records and involved with the production of Bill Haley and the Comets and their hit record, *'Rock Around the Clock'*. He also started and ran Frank Sinatra's Reprise records, the original vanity label designed exclusively for Frank. Reprise was a division of Warner Brothers. Jay then became President of ABC / Dunhill Records, releasing singles and albums by artists such as Steppenwolf, Tom Petty, Three Dog Night, Jim Croce and Steely Dan. When MCA bought out the ABC label in 1979, Jay became president of Ariola, only to leave a year later and go to Motown.

Dennis Katz, our attorney, negotiated the distribution deal with Jay Lasker for the new Kreiner Cossie label. We were going to use our initials and call the label KC records but thought it would be confused with KC and the Sunshine Band. We then agreed, since we were basing the label on the West Coast, we would call our new label Ocean Ariola Records. This way the Germans from Ariola would also have their international branding as well as our Ocean brand. Our next step was the design of the label.

Marc had one concept in mind, and I had other ideas. We each agreed to come up with a design and whoever had the best-looking design would prevail.

I was in LA setting up our office with Marc and got a call from Larry Douglass. You may recall Larry's name from Chapter Five. He conducted my tour of RCA. Larry was now running Epic Records West Coast operation. He had a new release coming out and wanted Marc and I to work on the record in the clubs. After our meeting with Larry at Epic, Marc had to go meet with his graphic designer regarding the new label. Marc was on a mission to get his label design in the works, and I didn't have a clue as to what my Ocean design would be.

Larry asked if I could join him for lunch in Westwood with two artists on his label. As it was always great to see Larry, and I felt I owed him for all he had done during my earlier days, naturally I said yes.

It turned out Larry was having lunch with the two singers from the group Heart, Ann and Nancy

Wilson. The ladies were charming, very knowledgeable about the music business and a variety of subjects. During those conversations I mentioned I had recently seen artwork from either one of their albums covers or some magazine covers. I described the artwork saying, "It was a musical note flying through the air and looked like it was about to land on one side of a seesaw. On the side of the seesaw touching the ground, was a red resting heart, waiting for that note to lift it into the air". I told them I thought it was a cool concept and asked if they designed that piece of artwork. They informed me the artist lived in their hometown, Seattle. He obviously was extremely talented, it was his concept, and they used him for their magazine and press artwork. I asked for the phone number, as I was about to launch a new record company and needed a label design. The luncheon with Larry and the two talented and charming sisters was both enjoyable and productive. As Marc had already begun working on the new label design, I proceeded to contact the Wilson Sisters recommendation, Loren Salazar.

The next day I was back in New York, and called Loren, told him about my lunch with the Wilson sisters, then described my vision for Ocean Records. Keep in mind this was 1979 and you listened to music on your record player which consisted of a turntable and tone arm with a needle at the end playing a vinyl disc. Sounds primitive by today's standards, but it worked just fine for decades

My concept for the label was a scene along the horizon with a large tonearm extending out into the Ocean as if the needle was playing the Ocean water like it was a record.

We had a good exchange of ideas, and he sent me pictures of some of his previous works. This guy was good, and I could see why the ladies from Heart were so supportive. He mentioned he planned on coming to New York to visit some of the art galleries. He gave me his travel dates, and I told him my driver Pete would pick him up from the airport and take him to the Plaza. I would take care of his expenses as payment in advance for doing our label artwork. The plan was, when he got back to Seattle, he would follow my concept and deliver the label rendering within a week.

Since Marc and I were in a bit of a competition and both were eager to get our label up and running, this process couldn't come soon enough. Prior to Loren's departure he showed me other limited-edition pieces of art that he had created. I was so impressed I purchased ten different pieces of original art, signed and numbered, from him.

As promised, the following week the artwork arrived. I was thrilled! Loren delivered what I felt was a beautiful piece of inspired art. My exuberance soon turned to grief. Upon closer examination of this artwork, which was intended to serve as a record label, it becomes clear that incorporating a large central hole for a 45 rpm record changer, or even a smaller hole for an album, would significantly compromise the integrity of the design. I loved this art; I couldn't come to grips with destroying the piece.

I called Loren and told him about my dilemma; I did not want to deface his work. He understood and thanked me for my hospitality. He also said thanks by sending me the original art along with one hundred signed and numbered copies of this beautiful work. If you want to truly see the talents of Loren Salazar, go to his website www.lorensalazar.com you will see hundreds of examples of his works. I'm glad sales websites weren't a thing in 1979 otherwise, instead of purchasing only ten pieces of art, I would have purchased 100.

We needed to give the Ocean label an identity. We had three recording projects in the studio and didn't have a final label design. I have to admit, Marc's concept was almost equally outstanding and he seemed to have the foresight to know, both a large hole and small hole would need to be part of the label art. Marc's version made the most sense. It looked worked well for the 45 and LP center holes. The final version of Marcs entry put Ocean Ariola America, on the top section of the life preserver, leaving the center open.

When Marc and I launched this label, we mapped out a diverse roster of experienced singers and musicians that would give us a fair shot in a crowded playing field. We experimented with talent from different areas in the entertainment business.

Marc had many contacts in Hollywood and during our first year of operation we recorded film actors Ann Margaret, Paul Sabu and Burt Young. We also signed more traditional artists like Ullanda McCullough, David Williams and James Jamerson, aka, Chanson.

Ullanda was Valerie Simpson's backup singer when Nick and Val, aka Ashford & Simpson performed live. David Williams and James Jamerson, Jr. were an amazing guitar and bass duo, similar to the great musicianship of Nile and Bernard from Chic.

Chanson is a French word meaning song. One of the two musicians who comprised the group Chanson was, James Jamerson Jr., an amazing bass player who followed in his father's footsteps. We all referred to Junior's father as Pops. He was the bass foundation for the famous Funk Brothers from Detroit, who were the studio house band for Motown. Pops Jamerson played bass on over 100 hit records by: The Four Tops, Temptations, Junior Walker, Steve Wonder, Marvin Gaye and every other Motown artist who recorded in Detroit. James Junior took over from Pops and became a popular studio base player in Los Angeles. Junior Jamerson recorded and toured with Bob Dylan, The Temptations and Travares. The rhythm section on our debut Chanson album featured Jeff Picaro on drums.

(Jeff was the drummer and member of the hit group Toto.)

The rest of the rhythm section of Chanson was James Jamerson Jr. on Bass, and David Williams on Guitar. David played lead guitar on Michael Jackson's *Off The Wall* album and played with Michael on the 1981 international tour. Some of his noteworthy guitar parts can be heard in the song *'Billy Jean'* on the Thriller Album, as well as the guitar tracks he put down on *'Bad'*, and *'Smooth Criminal'* off the *BAD* Album. David Williams also recorded albums with Madona, The Pointer Sisters, and a host of other big-name artists. David was a true talent who always preferred to be behind the scenes.

We recorded two albums and released the single *'Don't Hold Back',* from Chanson's debut album which reached 21 on the R&B charts and top 10 on the dance charts. Despite working with great musicians, achieving a number one hit was often an elusive goal. Marc and I contributed in the promotion of many major hits, but identifying the exact recipe for a chart-topping song was no easy task.

We dedicated ourselves to supporting our artists and formed professional relationships with many of them. David Williams distinguished himself as an exceptionally skilled guitarist. He was not only talented but also demonstrated kindness and humility, qualities that are uncommon among most recording artists. We developed a strong sense of connection with David, particularly during challenging times.

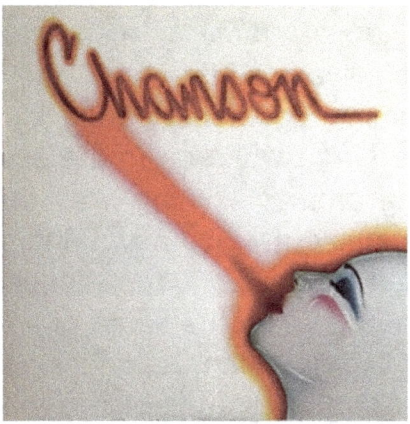

He experienced the unfortunate loss of a parent, which left him deeply distressed. Consequently, I accompanied him on a flight to his home in Newport News, Virginia.

Michael and David Williams
Photo credit John Isaac

I was invited to stay in the family home with about 30 other family members for the weekend-long wake. They say food always brings a family together. Around 5:00 am on Saturday morning I woke up to the scent of the most enticing aromas coming from the kitchen downstairs. I made my way down and saw three elderly women commanding the kitchen. An aunt was keeping an eye on the sauté of ham hocks, onions, and garlic. One neighbor lady was chopping red and green bell peppers and Grandma was starting to stack up three to four large collard green leaves pulled from what looked like an overflowing bushel of greens. Grandma saw me standing in the doorway just sniffing and said, "Well don't just stand there, wash your hands and put on this apron."

For the next few hours, before anyone else got up, I was assigned to the collard green detail. I was shown how to clean and stack the rich green leaves four deep and to cut down and across. Once my greens dicing mission was accomplished, a second wave of chefs came in and took over for the rest of the morning. The kitchen became an extended version of Beat Bobby Flay but without time limits. However, in this episode the multiple chefs were cooking for over 100 soon to be taste testers, opposed to two or three food judges.

At the wake, I encountered a friend that David

and I both knew, Everett 'Blood' Hollins. Blood was the man who brought the Chic demo to me a few years earlier at Buddah Records. Blood always seemed to be working on recording projects, and I realized he must have met both David Williams, as well as Nile Rodgers as studio secession players.

Over my years in the music business, I've attended numerous funerals. Although this weekend wake was sad, it was simultaneously a celebratory occasion. David's mom brought the kid up right, and he and his family were living testimony to that decency. That weekend I learned the true meaning of the phrase, '*The fruit doesn't fall too far from the tree.'* Everyone in his family seemed to share the same qualities of decency, kindness, and family.

Marc and I felt that a major rollout party for Ocean would make an impact on the LA market. Our MK Plaza Hotel party from the previous year in New York City seemed to work out great and figured a West Coast version would work equally as well for Ocean Ariola Records. We hired a top Hollywood PR firm, Rogers and Cowan, that represented half of the actors and sports figures living in LA. Hollywood was famous for having noteworthy events, from launching new movie releases to entertainers getting their star cemented in the sidewalk on Hollywood Boulevard.

We wanted a special location so our point person, publicist Ramon Hervey II, suggested The

Marian Davies mansion on U.S. Highway 1 in Santa Monica. You may know of her. Marian was an up-and-coming starlet who at a young age became the mistress to William Randolph Hearst. The mistress occupation seemed to have its perks; her home was opulent. We felt this was a perfect location. A mansion directly on the ocean with a large private beach. It was a beautiful home with a sizeable outside courtyard area which could accommodate up to 400 guests, as was labeled legal for occupancy. Record World Magazine reported that the number of industry professionals attending our event was significantly higher than the recommended legal limit.

Marc and I had made all the arrangements to pull off the Plaza party, but Hollywood was special, we required the help from the crew at Rogers and Cowin. Bill Wardlow, the chart editor of Billboard Magazine, along with the mayor of

LA presented Marc and I with the keys to the city. I remember leaning over on the stage and telling Bill, "I don't know if giving the keys to the city to Marc is such a good idea. I hope all the businesses have double locks on their doors."

In the afternoon of our event, we had a dump truck deposit a mountain of ice on the beach to chill champagne. Our PR people were in charge of the invites which included their A list. Marc, Jay Lasker and I made the record industry list. Our one special request, we wanted a marching band with little people to make a grand entrance ahead of Marc and my arrival. Rogers and Cowin had the Santa Monica marching band fronting a procession onto the ground and leading the band into the courtyard was my all-time favorite little person, Billy Barty, with eight of his compadres marching behind him.

In the courtyard out front there were two guest entry stations which had a group of models dressed as sailors escorting people to a photo station where two large Ocean logos were positioned so you could look through the center hole and get a picture surrounded by our logo. Once again, bravo to Marc's label choice.

Of course, for this event we had a DJ who played some of our new tracks, many of Chic's hits, and other artists' records associated with our companies. We invited every artist we worked with; of course, they all showed. Rogers and Cowan delivered a star filled list of at least 30 celebrities to enjoy the party. The Stars showed up in force. Actors like Peter Falk from Columbo fame and Dudley Morre and Don Johnson. Alongside Sports figures like Wilt Chamberlin and Dorothy Hamil, actors Ann Margaret, Burt Young, Nile Rodger, and Elliot Gould were in attendance. Heather Locklear, and others mingled with celebrity musicians and record company executives from both New York City and Los Angeles.

There was a sign in the courtyard that said occupancy 400, but I believe more like 800 attended. There were three open bars and three food stations scattered on the beach and in the courtyard, and the paparazzi were everywhere. This turned out to be a great launch party. Several days after the party, Ramon told us there were more limousines coming and going from this party than he had ever seen. The LAPD had to turn US 1, The Pacific Coast Highway, into one lane and direct traffic for five hours. As I recall, we were billed quite heavily for that traffic jam inconvenience.

Peter Falk and Dudley Moore and friends
(Photo by Richard Creamer/Michael Ochs
Archives/Getty Images)

*Elliot Gould, Nile Rodgers, a guest,
Tom Cossie, Sidney Miller and Dorothy Hamil*

Peter Falk "Columbo", Burt Young, aka
"Pauly from Rocky" & Cossie

Columbo Telling Cossie he has guilt written all over his face.

OCEAN RECORDS BOWS WITH A BASH

Marc Krainer and Tom Cossie hosted a gala extravaganza recently to celebrate the christening of their new record label, Ocean Records and Mayor Tom Bradley of the Los Angeles proclaimed May 22 "Ocean Records Day" in the city. Over 800 guests, including numerous celebrities and industry notables, were treated to a customized disco sound and light show at the Sand and Sea Club. Ocean also introduced its first artist, Ullanda (who performed "Stars" and "Want Ads" from her forthcoming album, "Love Zone") and Burt Young (who introduced his single, "Burt's Blues," on which he plays trumpet).Shown at the party are top row, from left: Kreiner; Jay Lasker, president of Ariola Records; Cossie,; Howard Stark, vice president of Ariola; Mrs. Jack Forsythe; Record Worlds Jack Forsythe; David Williams of Chanson; Kreiner, Lee Bailey, KUTE radio; (bottom row) Peter and Shera Falk; Kreiner; Ullanda; Burt Young; Cossie Ullanda as she performs at the party

RECORD WORLD JUNE 9, 1979

We wanted our Ocean Records roster to feature a female vocalist. She had to be attractive, articulate, have a great personality, have touring experience and, most of all, have a great voice. Almost all the great female vocalist who launched solo careers started off working as studio background singers, learning their chops. They would then tour with a major artist sharing harmonies, lead lines, and singing backup. Ullanda did all of the above. Her most notable role to me was her backup work with Ashford and Simpson. My favorite song by Nick and Val was, *'Solid, Solid as a Rock'*. I loved their records. I always thought they were the best female/male duo in the business. Ullanda also did background work on records for Quincy Jones, Bette Midler, Tina Turner, and Diana Ross. She also worked with my all-time favorite background singer- turned star lead vocalist, Luther Vandross.

As a side story, please let me make a point about working your way to the top by paying your dues. It would always put a smile on my face when I heard Luther sing. Luther sang background on the first three Chic albums. He was amazing from his childhood to his passing. Nile would tell the story about Luther in grade school and high school.

He said, "When there was a talent show, all the musicians would practice for weeks. I would practice hard for months and play my song on guitar for the contest. When we each performed our numbers in the school auditorium, everyone would politely applaud. Then, when Luther played and started singing, all the girls in the school auditorium would swoon, 'OOOH Luther!"

I could envision that performance clearly, Luther doing that little gymnastic vocal run with the girls swooning, 'OOOH Luther'. Nile said, "We hated Luther at that time." He obviously was that good even back when he was a young kid.

This next story is but a side bar, to a side bar, and has nothing to do with anything musically significant, but about Luther's physical agility.

Every artist who has had R&B radio success wants the same attention on pop radio and also wants their record label to give them the same spending budgets that the pop artists would receive. R&B artists also wanted to play the same venues as Pop and Rock artists. After all, most R&B records that crossed over to pop sold just as many records, as the pop artists, but were not always treated the same regarding financial support. Chic wanted that venue crossover experience as well, and decided to play The Roxy, one of the two primary rock clubs on Sunset Strip. The other key rock club on Sunset was The Whiskey a Go Go.

It took place during the first Chic album. Luther, Lucy, and Norma Jean were singing background for this gig. Luther's weight always fluctuated. You would either see the 250 pound heavy Luther, or the 180 pound Luther. The weight never seemed to impact his amazing vocals. Luther always sounded great no matter his weight.

Chic wanted to play for a rock crowd. Nile, Bernard, and Tony were a Rock Trio prior to forming Chic. We booked the Roxy. We were at soundcheck, and the side stage door was open so the roadies could bring in the band's equipment. A few of us were standing around a table with two chairs in the dimly lit area just in front of the stage. The only bright light was coming in from that open stage door. All of a sudden, a not so large black and white dog ran into the club through the stage door. Luther spotted the dog and to everyone's amazement, Luther did a standing jump, straight up and did a perfect landing on one of the chairs. Unbeknownst to us, Luther was deathly afraid of dogs and wouldn't come down from the chair until the dog was herded out of the club. I only mention this because I'd never seen a 280-pound man—other than watching the NFL football combine—jump straight up that high in the air and, in Luther's case, stick the perfect landing. The show did go on. The packed room loved Chic, and Luther kept a keen eye focused on that stage door.

Meanwhile, Marc and I were fans and released Ullanda's first album, *Love Zone*, in 1979. It was produced by Bernard Drayton, Leon Pendarvis, and George McMahon. Her first single 'Love Zone' made it into the top 30 on the charts and the album entered the Top 100.

Congrats for Ullanda

Following Ullanda's recent appearance at Leviticus in New York, the Ocean Records recording artist was congratulated by an all-star lineup of sister performers. Seen standing, in front, from left are Valerie Simpson, Norma Jean, Lucy Martin of Chic; seated are Ullanda and Phyllis Hyman.

When I mentioned Ocean signed a diverse group of talent, I do mean diverse. There was Burt Young who played Pauly in the Rocky films, superstar actress Ann Margaret, and a talented guitar player and producer named Paul Sabu. Paul's dad was the star Indian actor who appeared in just about every India centric movie made in the 1930's and 40's. *Elephant Boy, Thief of Bagdad and Jungle Book* to name a few. When in LA I would have lunch with Paul at one of his favorite eateries on Sunset Blvd., The Old World Restaurant. Back in the late 1970's every location on Sunset was a landmark. Take The Old World Restaurant. If you didn't know it's location, anyone could tell you, 'Oh! It's directly across the street from Spago's and Tower Records'. If you ever spent any time in LA and didn't know any of these landmarks, well, then you didn't know LA very well at all.

Paul's talents were evident both on stage and in the studio. Marc and I concurrently had a deal with MCA when we rolled out our Ocean Ariola label. For Ocean Records, Marc worked with Paul and produced several top dance 12-inch singles for Ann Margaret.

Paul then produced Sister Power, and Debbie Jacobs, as well as writing and producing 'High On Your Love', a top 70 chart single in Billboard's Hot 100 chart and number one on the Dance Charts. Paul Sabu was as interesting a man as he was talented. Our lunch meeting conversations centered around his proud family history and his concerns about life and longevity. Paul was a health freak, no drugs just heavy doses of vitamins. He would tell me stories about his grandfather who was a *Mahout* (an elephant trainer) in India. His Dad, Selar Sabu, started as a child star in Hollywood as "Sabu" the Elephant Boy, and after a series of successes in films during World War II joined the Air Force as a tail gunner in a B-24 bomber and was awarded The Flying Cross Medal of Honor. Every lunch at The Old World restaurant would end with Paul popping a hand full of vitamins. He was a young, healthy, good looking kid living a clean lifestyle. So, I asked, "Why all the vitamins?" He told me his family did not live long lives and his goal was to live longer than his dad who died at 39. I remember those luncheons to this day. One of the reasons being that at one lunch I noticed him taking six niacin tablets. He told me it was good for his energy. He then offered me three tablets saying that it was plenty as I was just a vitamin beginner. I figured, what could it hurt? I'd seen niacin listed on multivitamin bottles as an acceptable ingredient. I took those three tablets with my traditional drink of mocha coffee. We went our separate ways and by the time I got back to the office in Beverly Hills I thought my head was going to explode. Walking into the office, our receptionist said, "What the hell happened to you? Your face and neck are beet red." She added, "Were you hanging out with Sabu". Apparently when most artists would share a doobie on the way to a restaurant or a pop of blow, it was a well-known inner office fact that Paul was offering vitamins.

Our short 14 month run at Ocean Ariola came to an end when Jay Lasker left and went over to Motown Records. Marc decided to stay with our newly formed record production deal at MCA Records and move a few of our former Ocean acts over to MCA to strike a deal on his own.

Ann Margaret with Marc Kreiner
(Photo by Steve Schapiro/Corbis via Getty Images)

I returned to New York City, moved back into my Sheffield apartment, and activated Record Logic Productions and Precision Records. I then signed Ullanda to Atlantic Records in 1981, and the Main Ingredient back to their original label RCA. It had been ten years since I promoted The Main Ingredients first hit records when I worked at RCA. This time I signed the group under the Record Logic production brand. I can't emphasize enough the importance of leaving a company amicably, respectfully, and supportively, no matter the circumstances of your departure. It all comes back full circle. In chapter seventeen I tell the story of being fired from RCA. Ten years later I was back signing groups to that label. Once again, it always pays to leave your former employer in good graces.

Chapter Twenty-Two

The Sheffield, Record Logic & Precision Records

When Marc and I decided to go our own ways, I relocated back to my New York City office apartment at 322 West 57th Street. The building is known as The Sheffield. This was always my home away from my Pittsburgh home. Back in 1978 when MK and Chic were hitting the charts, I was flush with cash and signed a nine-year lease, at a bargain price, to occupy a large apartment on the 42nd floor. New York City real estate at that time was in a slump, which forced a renter's market. There were numerous high rise apartment buildings all over Manhattan that were half occupied. I lived in this new almost completely developed building and requested the highest floor that had water and electricity. That may sound like an odd request but though the building's elevators would go all the way to the top floor, only floors 1 through 22 had completed apartments. The 42nd floor was the highest with utilities and some infrastructure. My corner apartment had a great view to the southeast overlooking Time Square, the World Trade Centers and Statue of Liberty. Looking west I had a full view of The Hudson River and most of the

West Side. The development company was thrilled with my offer. I proposed a nine-year lease, so they built out my apartment and had it move-in ready within two weeks of signing the lease.

The day of moving was a true event. Not one to procrastinate, I furniture shopped, marathon style, at Bloomingdales and in one hour bought six rooms of furniture. One week later when they delivered the furniture, I was told the inside freight elevator was not operating but they mentioned the outside construction supply lifts would work if I could find an operator after construction hours. My Fleetwood Limousine drivers Pete and Eddy came to the rescue. Riding up and down on an open outside elevator with numerous loads of furniture was an experience, especially for Pete who was terrified of heights. We ended up taking Vodka shot breaks at Patsy's bar between each elevator load. The apartment ended up looking great and, oh, what a view!

The Sheffield was a great location I could walk out the front of my building turn left and within 200 feet on West 56th Street were two of my favorite restaurants, Patty's and Di Angelos, side by side. I felt like I hit the restaurant numbers. I loved my island apartment. I say island because I had the only completed apartment above the 22nd floor in the entire building. It was quite shocking to people who visited me for a meeting. The lobby was upscale with spacious seating areas, a 24-hour concierge desk, and two double banks of high-speed elevators. If you pressed the button for floor 42, when the door opened there were light bulbs hanging from the ceiling and three corridors of unfinished walls. As you would walk around the corner and down along one of those corridors to my apartment at the end, you would see doors secured by chains, preventing entrance to all of the unfinished apartments. I say unfinished because not even drywall had been delivered to those apartments. My new apartment was the only one completely built out between the 22nd and 50th floors. At night, walking to my front door, you could hear and feel the wind blowing through those open window spaces and front door openings where the key locks and door handles would go. On a cold windy night, with the hallways only half lit by bare bulbs hanging from wires, the lights provided moving shadows while whistling winds blew through the door openings orchestrating cool but haunting visuals and harmonies.

There was a TV series starring Daren McGavin called The Night Stalker. During those early construction days as I walked the hallways to my apartment, I would think about Carl Kolchak walking down half lit hallways in abandoned buildings in pursuit of blood sucking vampires.

After a short walk, my epic horror journey would end when opening my front door to an elegantly appointed apartment with a great view of the city.

I truly miss those days living in the city. This building was popular with the entertainment industry. I would run into members of Bruce Springsteen's E-Street band and a host of Broadway actors who resided at The Sheffield. On one occasion, while Tookie, Michael Jackson's manager, and Michael, were staying across town at The Helmsley Palace, they discovered there was a scam happening at their expense. Leona Helmsley, taking advantage of Michael's star status, sold tickets for tables to the highest bidder to get a look at Michael while he stayed at her hotel.

Tookie got wind of this enterprise and told me Micheal didn't seem to mind the attention at first. He was used to gawkers wherever he went, he assumed it was just more of the same. That was until one group of tourists, having dinner at a table across from Michael's, thought they didn't get enough "Michael time" during their dinner and felt cheated. Michael was not aware Leona's grifting was taking place. Michael got pissed when he discovered the hotel restaurant's tables were being sold with the promise of meeting him. Tookie also figured it out, lost his temper with Leona, and immediately moved Michel out of the hotel over to my apartment for a few days. Tookie used my place when I was in Los Angeles, so it was an easy and convenient move. This was also a comfortable location with fellow theatrical people in the building. There was no chance of getting ambushed by irate fans at the Sheffield.

Over the years, my New York City apartment functioned as convenient and complimentary accommodations for numerous artists. During our recording with Epic Records, Pittsburgh recording artist David Werner was a frequent guest, often taking liberties with my generous supply of Perrier Jouet Champaigne.

In the remaining years of my lease at The Sheffield, the apartment would serve as the headquarters for Precision Records, Record Logic, and Saturn Records. Record Logic was my production company through which I signed Michael Wycoff to RCA.

Three years after our Ocean Ariola Records release of *Love Zone* in 1979, two additional albums were recorded with *Ullanda McCullough*. Ullanda toured with Ashford and Simpson for several years, and in 1981, producers Nick Ashford and Valerie Simpson produced the self-titled album, Ullanda McCullough. This album included two singles that reached the middle of the charts: *'You'll Never Know'*, and *'Bad Company'*.

Bert DeCoteaux produced her second album with Atlantic, entitled *Watching You Watching Me*.

Though we had only one R&B chart single, Nick and Val delivered a strong album. The duo wrote strong material for this album, did an amazing job in production, yet still only delivered two mid chart singles

Record Logic also facilitated the return of The Main Ingredient to their original label, RCA. Previously, while working for RCA, I promoted their records *'Everybody Plays the Fool'* and *'Just Don't Want To Be Lonely'*. On this occasion, the group was signed under the Record Logic production brand.

As mentioned, several times, I cannot emphasize the importance of how you leave a company can affect future relationships. Departing respectfully helps preserve connections—even if you're let go. I was fired from RCA, yet ten years later, I was signing groups to that same label. Leaving on good terms always pays off.

Compared to the Main Ingredient's success in the early 1970's this release in the early 1980's did not have a single that made the charts, though it was an equally well-produced album.

I often remind myself that even with top producers, musicians, and a strong lead vocalist, chart success isn't guaranteed. I've worked on many promising projects that didn't become hits.

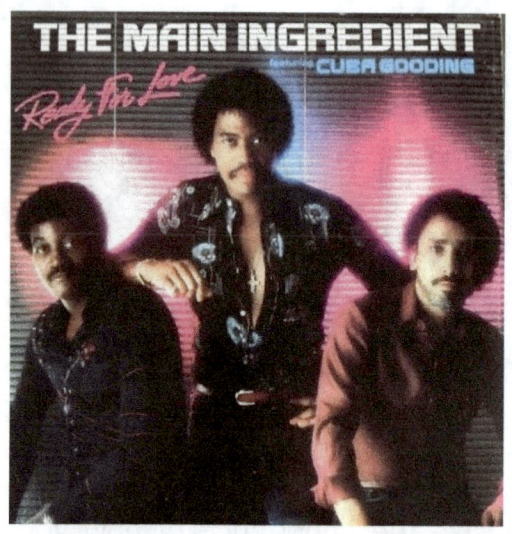

In truth, no one can predict outcomes in the music industry, it's unpredictable, and not for the faint-hearted.

Further examples of great talent with outstanding production were best represented by the talented R&B song stylist, Michael Wycoff. Between 1981 and 1983, RCA released three albums through Record Logic Productions. In 1981 *Come To My World* was a masterfully produced project by Grammy award winner, and, jazz vocalist, Steve Tyrell. The single released on this debut album was a compelling duet with Michael and vocalist, Mary Clayton. You may remember Mary Clayton's distinctive voice from singing a duet with Mick Jagger on the Rolling Stones single, *'Gimme Shelter'*. Not a bad credential to have on your first single to be released, entitled *'One Alone'*. Though critically acclaimed, we had little chart success in the states and minimal activity in England and Germany.

For Michael Wycoff's next two albums, we decided to try a different production direction and went with arranger and jazz producer Webster Lewis. Once again, both of these albums included a cast of the best studio players in Los Angeles including Herbie Hancock. All three albums had great sounding singles releases, though again, with only minimal chart success.

Saturn Records - Prime Time Music Precision Records – Record Logic

I always wanted to have a record label named after a planet. Mercury was taken, Pluto sounded too dog-like, and Uranus Records would have become the brunt of stupid ass jokes. Therefore, it had to be Saturn. Or as one tag line was recommended, 'If it's not Saturn, It's Uranus'.

Having initially spent four years with independent distribution then five years with direct distribution at RCA, I decided to take a shot again with the Independents. . In 1983, several independent distributors continued to operate after the departure of major labels. Red Distribution was among these distributors, managing promotion, marketing, and sales activities. For smaller labels such as Saturn, operational responsibilities would include talent acquisition, pre-production, booking studio time, equipment cartage, recording the sessions, mixing the tracks, mastering, artwork and packaging, manufacturing, inventory management, and preparing marketing materials for the release of the completed singles, albums, and CDs. Considering the expense to complete just one album project, all in costs would be between $150,000 and $200,000 just to bring a project to the market.

At which point the financial expenditure involved in promotion and marketing would be the next step. Saturn did make a major commitment to many artists. It was standard practice for small companies like Saturn Records, as well as a lot of major labels, to have your people scout talent. Major record labels had an A&R department and a staff of scouts who would travel the country and visit live venues where bands played, looking for that special artist who captivated the crowd. as the president and owner of Saturn Records; or any small company trying to compete with the major labels was either an act of courage or a blatant act of stupidity. I often times felt like the latter, and in reflection would refer to myself as "The Village Idiot", for taking the risk. If the artist was unique or had a great following at the local clubs, the next item on the checklist would be, did the singer or group have good, original material. The more hit-record-sounding original songs in their repertoire the better. Unless the artist was performing original material, there would be little interest in signing the act.

Unknown artists who closely mimicked popular acts were labeled cover bands. Don't get me wrong, cover bands are great, and people pack the clubs to see them because they already know all the popular songs and club owners are happy to book them. The objective is to get the crowds in and keep them there for all three sets of music so they can sell alcohol.

Nine out of ten times when a friend, who was not familiar with the business, would say, "You have to see this band, they sound just like band X that's on the radio." I would reply, "If they sound like, and play all the songs just like, the original artist, why would anyone buy their record when the original is out there and available". There were some exceptions to that rule. If a band had a unique arrangement to a former hit song, that was truly different from the original, it would sometimes work. In one case, I recorded a band, Diamond Reo. They were a local Pittsburgh band who did a unique version of the song *"Ain't That Peculiar"* which had been a hit on Motown Records by the soul stylist, Marvin Gaye. This was noteworthy as this unknown group made it into the top 50 on Billboard's Hot 100 pop chart with a cover tune.

Over the years, and continuing through the late 1980's, I 've worked on over fifty projects and collaborated with a wide range of artists. Some of these artists signed with major record labels through my production and management company Record Logic. Prime Time Music was a label designated for rock projects, featuring artists such as King Creole, Joe Stark, and Modern Man. Several other artists and projects remained under the Saturn Label brand, including George Romero's film soundtrack album *The Day of the Dead*, soul singers Floyd Beck, The Exotic Birds, Sputzy Sparacino, Joe Granito, The Klass, Sun Factor Six, and the Philadelphia Acapella group, The Foundation.

Precision Records operated out of my Sheffield apartment on 57th Street in New York City. The label released both Silencers albums, *Rock and Roll Enforcers* and *Romanic*, which were distributed through the CBS Label Group. Due to scheduling conflicts, Bobby Clearmountain was unavailable to produce *Romanic*, the second Silencer album on Precision. Given the band's history with their previous project, it was decided I would record a second album. I booked studio time at Media Sound, enlisting a great support team with background vocalists Jocelyn Brown and Krystal Davis, as well as Lyonel Jobe on steel drums and the David Letterman studio show band director, Bruce Kapler for horn solos and arrangements. Although this production was noteworthy, it only achieved limited radio play. The *Romanic* album featured two singles: 'Sidewalk Romeo' with lead vocal's by Frank Czuri, and a reggae-inspired track also written by Frank Czuri, titled 'Cry Tough'.

In the early to mid 80's, I produced numerous projects at Media Sound. The studio was built in an old, abandoned church and was my go-to studio in New York City. It was convenient, being just across the street from The Sheffield, and along with Power Station and Hit Factory, was one of the best recording facilities in New York City.

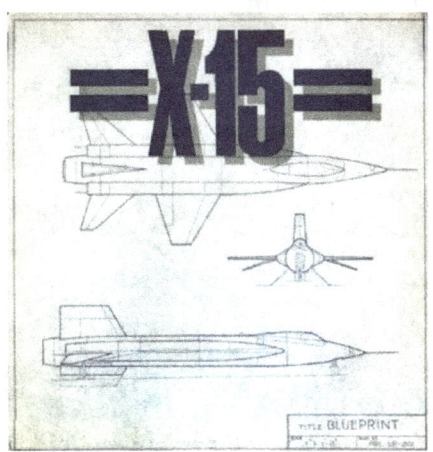

In 1982, Media Sound experienced a productive year in collaboration with my label, Precision Records. I co-produced the rock band X 15, working alongside band members T. Doverspike and David Cross. One notable member of the group, keyboardist Jim Blazer, continued his musical career following the disbandment of X 15. He toured internationally with renowned rock artist Chuck Berry and subsequently dedicated two decades to performing on the Hammond B3 organ with The Spencer Davis Group.

It was Stevie Winwood who originally recorded the iconic B3 parts on the group's major hits: *Gimme Some Lovin'* and *I'm a Man*. Over the span of twenty years, it is likely that Jim performed these classics countless times, whether concluding regular sets or as part of the group's encore performances.

Jim Blazer is living proof there is life beyond playing in a rock & roll band. While all this music was going on, he was also a successful financial planner, operating his company, Wealth Planning Group, located in Santa Clarita, California, focusing on the well-being of fellow musicians. There are two quotes from musicians I know that I will always remember.

"A journey of a thousand miles does indeed begin with the first step" …Jim Blazer
"One chord is fine, two chords are pushing it, threechords and you're into Jazz" …. Lou Reed.

Graf, as you may remember, was a talented band from Warren, Ohio, that featured Frank Pellino on guitar and vocals, drummer extraordinaire Jose Ortiz, bassist Tim Graziano, (all former members of the I Don't Care band). Graf also featured Peter Tokar on keys and vocals. Both X15 and Graf released their debut albums on Precision.

The name *Graf* had long fascinated me. I'd always been captivated by the Graf Zeppelin, that majestic, ridged, cigar-shaped airship from the early 1930's. More than five decades ago, I tried to convince my wife to let me name our son Graf.

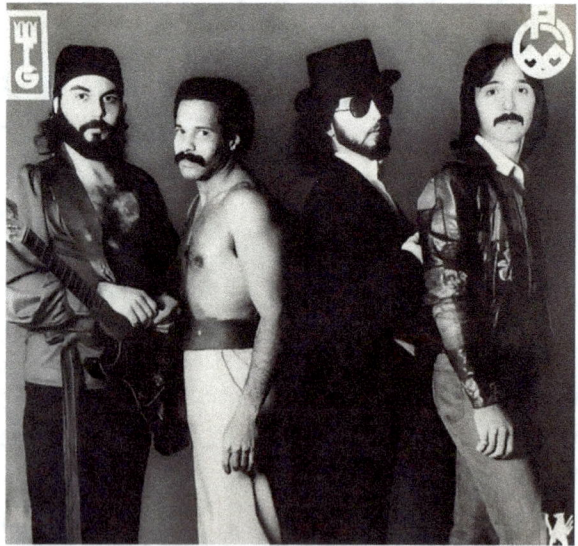

That idea didn't exactly get off the ground, so we settled on *Eric*. Over the years, I made several playful attempts to persuade various relatives to christen their offspring *Graf*, but none of those efforts ever managed to ...wait for it...become airborne.

Finally, when the I Don't Care Band disbanded, I floated the name *Graf* to the newly formed, talented foursome out of Cleveland. To my delight and surprise, they embraced it. The name had finally found its place, and besides, *Zeppelin* had already been taken.

Cleveland was always a hot spot for talent, and I had remained friends with agents, managers, and promoters dating back to my regional promotion man days with RCA in the late 60's. Mark Litton and Jim Quinn were two booking agents and managers who knew the market and over the years either managed or booked the groups: I Don't Care, Graf, Champion and Exotic Birds.

The I Don't Care Band really didn't care about hit singles and only would play original, most of which were not pop or commercial sounding compositions. One of the only non-original songs they did perform was the Jimmy Hendrix classic song entitled *'Fire'*. I signed this band to Buddah/ Kama Sutra Records, based upon Quinn's ability to tour the group and and knowing the bands manager, a true music business character, Pete Knapp. Upon hearing their version of *'Fire'*. I think that Jimmy Hendrix would have also been impressed with the I Don't Care Treatment of *'Let Me Stand Next to Your Fire'*.

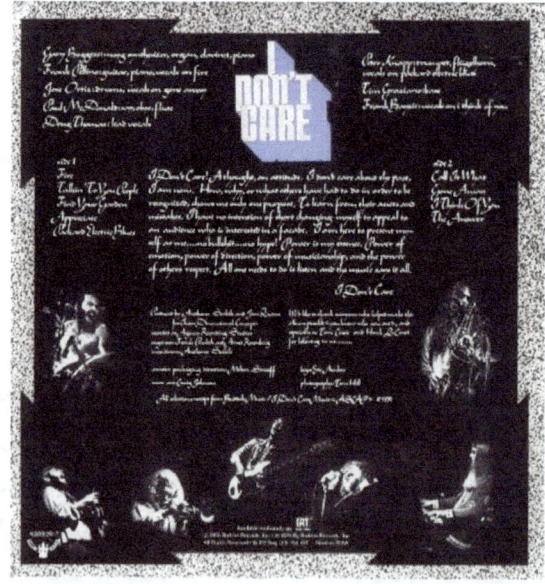

Jim Quinn Solar Management
Photo Credit Anastasia Pantsios

Ohio was always a great state for live entertainment and especially for cover bands. The drinking age, being only 18, also didn't hurt bar attendance. Every band who performed live always wanted to have their original music heard.

On the other hand, the bar and club owners' priority was to build crowds and sell alcohol. A great sounding cover band playing familiar dance music was always a drawing card, and the top of the deck in the Cleveland and Akron markets was an amazing cover band called Champion. You would consider this band, the other side of the coin compared to I Don't Care. As a comparison, Champion should have called themselves 'We Care A Lot'.

Champion were six talented pop rock musicians from Cleveland. When they performed it was not unusual to see an abundance of great looking girls swooning over the band.

John Norman second from the end with the tallest hair
Photo Credit Kathie Hirko .

And, of course, guys always followed the girls. The club owners loved these guys and the drinking crowd they pulled. No mystery why the local clubs and bar owners voted Champion the best local band in Ohio.

Jim Quinn worked for Solar Management, owned by Otto Neuber, an older German American. Otto treated his artists like unworthy subjects and employees and would address them like a drill Sargent would discipline his recruits. I'll never forget meeting Otto at the Solar Management office in Beachwood Ohio, a southern suburb of Cleveland.

Jim Quinn was second in command in the office and Jim managed I Don't Care which I had recently signed to the Kama Sutra/ Buddah Records Label.

I was in Jim's office and heard a loud, bellowing voice call out from several offices away, "Kvinn, Ver ist da booking papers from last veek".

I asked Jim, "Was that Otto who I've heard so much about?"

Jim paused and said, "You must meet Otto, you are either going to love this guy or hate him."

Otto had been living in the states for years, but you would never have guessed that from his German accent and demeanor. Just recently I was trying to describe the Otto to Quinn relationship. I came up with this analogy. Picture yourself, viewing the Donald Trump meeting with Zelinsky when Donald was getting in Zelinsky's face regarding his lack of appreciation for all the claimed support Trump had given him. And there was Marco Rubio, sitting on the couch looking on in bewilderment, waiting for orders and the next course of action to embrace. Think of Otto as Trump and Quinn as Marco Rubio. It was obvious when dealing with the Solar Management artists, Otto would light the fire, fan the flames and Quinn oversaw putting the fires out, and making things work. Over the years I don't think I ever met a group that came out of that office that loved Otto or his approach to artist relations. Yet Quinn somehow survived the Supreme Leader's wrath.

I always had respect for Jim Quinn based upon the working conditions he was under and how he turned chaos into a more palatable situation.

Jim was also a musician and had played years earlier with a Cleveland band named Damnation of Adam Blessing. He had good ears, knew the business and when he asked me to come to Cleveland to see Champion, I did so without hesitation. I asked one of my friends, the bombastic John Bettencourt, who, at that time, was head of promotion at RCA, to accompany me on this trip to Cleveland. I played John a tape of several songs Jim had me record for Champion, one of which was an original composition, *'Dancing in the Dark'*. This song peaked Betancourt's interest enough, to fly in from New York. When he saw the crowd reaction at the club and heard the band's original songs blended in with all the popular cover tunes, he was sold. He told the group that when he got back to New York he would make sure the band would get signed to RCA.

The following week, some significant event must have transpired after his return to New York City. Rumor had it, Bettencourt was in a board meeting with one of the new, and ever-changing RCA Presidents, got into an altercation, and was fired. Therefore, with the new regime in play, the Champion deal went south. Shortly thereafter the lead singer of the band found God, decided to become a hairdresser, and John Norman the lead guitar player had to restructure his group.

When writing a book some forty plus years after the action occurred, it's difficult recalling the exact time frames and chain of events. I recently discovered there are noteworthy success stories in life after a band breaks up. Jimmy Blazer was one example and John Norman was another.

John Norman, once the lead guitarist for the regional rock band Champion, is living proof of a theory I've long held, that the same side of the brain used to master guitar scales and song structures also lends itself to entrepreneurship and strategic thinking. Whether or not science supports my theory, John's story certainly does.

After stepping off the stage, John transitioned seamlessly into another side of the world of live entertainment, joining the Cleveland based management team at Magicworks Entertainment. There, he helped orchestrate international tours for icons like David Copperfield, *Jesus Christ Superstar*, Fleetwood Mac, and Janet Jackson. However, it was in the world of exhibitions where he found his true passion. Over the past 25 years, John has built and sold multiple companies, successfully structuring deals with some of the world's largest entertainment conglomerates. He has produced blockbuster exhibitions seen by over 30 million people, including *Tutankhamun and the Golden Age of the Pharaohs, Titanic: The Artifact Exhibition, Cleopatra, St. Peter and the Vatican, Princess Diana - A Celebration, Pompeii, Michael Jackson, Real Pirates, Ramses the Great,* and *Machu Picchu.*

He is one of the few people in the world entrusted to tour history's most priceless artifacts, both from the depths of the sea and the sands of ancient civilizations.

With a rare blend of creativity, precision, and business acumen, John has transformed cultural storytelling into a global enterprise.

As we are now both residents of Southwest Florida, I recently had the pleasure of having lunch with John in Fort Myers. After seeing some of his exhibitions firsthand, I told him candidly, he's the one who should be writing a book.

John's proof and an example to all musicians, there is live after your band breaks up.

I signed the Exotic Birds to Saturn Records in 1983 and produced their first self-titled album at Beachwood Studios just south of Cleveland. I thought the group was unique, consisting of three percussion majors studying at the Cleveland Institute of Music. To capture the bands artistry, I commissioned a Disney graphic illustrator to develop a unique album cover to complement the musical trio.

The band's manager Mark Litton provided the final ingredient to help launch this band's career. Mark had a key contact with ICM, one of the nation's top concert booking agencies. Mark sent both the album and video to Bobby Brooks, the lead agent at ICM who represented a host of major artists. The group Culture Club was one of ICM's bands and they were riding high on the charts with two hit records, 'Do You Really Want to Hurt Me' and 'Karma Chameleon'. After listening to the Exotic

Birds album and watching the video, Bobby Brooks said the band would be a perfect fit and proposed a 60-city tour for the Exotic Birds as the opening act for Culture Club. This opportunity would have allowed the band to perform in major concert halls across the country, with audiences of approximately 20,000 at each event.

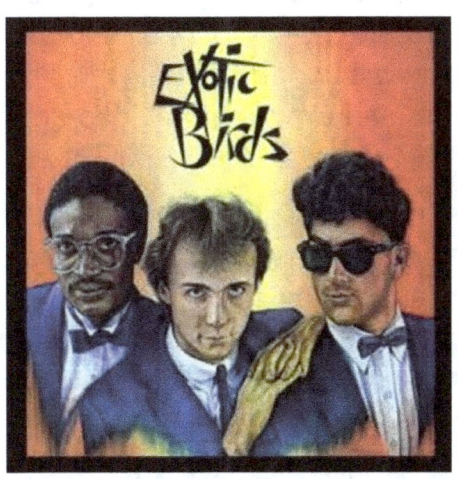

There was one standout song on this album entitled *'No Communication'*. This song reflected the story and times of human disinterest in each other, both socially and politically. A topic over 40 years ago that seems to be reminiscent of the social norms and politics of today. To capitalize on the moment, I hired a production company out of New York called Biggy Small Productions to produce a video. The video totally delivered the song's message. Saturn Records realized we needed to prepare for this event and build product inventory on both albums and cassettes. This would ensure there was sufficient product available for shipment to each market in support of the tour and meet potential sales demand.

This was turned out to be a potential dream situation, a great sounding album, a solid video, and a tour to complete the package. This was one of those 'let's roll the dice' moments. Saturn paid for all the packaging, recording, and travel costs in making the album and video, which resulted in taking out a loan to finish the video and building inventory.

What could possibly go wrong. To this day I do not know the answer to that question. The Exotic Birds did play the first two of 60 dates, then, for some unknown reason, determined they no longer wanted to continue, cancelled their tour dates, and broke up.

Recently I tracked down Mark Litton and found out over the past thirty years, he had been providing tour management, and tour accounting, for Metallica, Def Leppard, and Shaina Twain.

Writing this story about a project that nearly ruined me financially, I was extremely glad to speak with Mark. After years I finally got to ask him, "What the hell happened?" Mark told me he still didn't know, and the band members never provided answers.I spent months recording the album and not once did I see any drug use or heavy drinking.

Maybe that was their problem, every successful artist I knew at least smoked a little weed to cope with being on stage in front of 20,000 screaming fans. Mark said the band re-structured many times in the following years all to no avail. Maybe it was simply that threesome was not prepared for the grueling tour workload that was in store for them. Guess I'll never know.

In 1985 my New York City apartment complex, The Sheffield, decided to convert monthly rentals into condos for sale. I still had two years left on my lease, so they offered me a special rate to buy the unit. At that time, my finances were running low, and I didn't have the resources to purchase the apartment, so I moved my operation back to Pittsburgh.

A friend of mine, Gene Stevens, owned a textile company and warehouse located on Bigelow Blvd. between Pittsburgh and Oakland. He let me set up operations in a section of the building. To help cover my business expenses I took on independent promotion projects to recapitalize my record labels. Atlantic, Big Tree, RCA, and Mercury Records all provided me, and my old friend and independent promotion partner, Jack Forsythe, projects to promote and market their new releases in the Pittsburgh market.

Jack was living in Los Angeles and decided not to raise his family in the Hollywood environment. He wanted his children to attend school outside of the music industry setting. As a result, he moved with his wife, Romaine, and their two daughters back to Pittsburgh.

It took almost a year of promoting other record companies' projects to recoup and finance future project recording. My final album project in 1985 would be working with my film producer friend John Harrison on his latest project with Geroge A Romero, the soundtrack for *Day of The Dead*. John, several years earlier, produced and performed as a mad scientist in the Silencers video from the *Rock and Roll Enforcers* album. He told me Romero was looking for a label to release the soundtrack and John had recommended Saturn Records.

John had written most of the score for the film. He asked me if I would produce additional music for the album then release it on Saturn. I jumped at the opportunity and pulled together artists to write songs and perform on the album. Our plan was to incorporate our material along with his music scores to complete the soundtrack recording. I was asked to produce one side of the album with original material which opened the door to working with a new group of Pittsburgh musicians and singers. Sputzy Sparacino, the former lead singer of Pittsburgh's number one dance band Gigolo, wrote and performed the lead vocals on the songs; *'If Tomorrow Comes'* and *'The World Inside Your Eyes'*. Jim Blazer the keyboard player and arranger from the groups X15 and Modern Man, composed the song *'The Dead Walk'*. Our part of the soundtrack's music writing and production was a continuance of the theme composition and performance by John Harrison.

John was not a novice to the film and entertainment business, having directed over twenty films and wrote musical scores for numerous TV series like *The Creep Show* and *Tales from the Dark Side.*

It was a genuine pleasure working with John on this project.

Chart competition across all genres of music is notoriously intense, and the odds of a soundtrack album charting are slim to none without a hit single. The same rule that applies broadly to pop Billboard charted albums doubly rings true in this case. If there is no hit single, there is no hit album. Yet, amid this challenging landscape, one song from the soundtrack stood out to me with undeniable potential—*If Tomorrow Comes.*

Sputzy Sparacino wrote the song during the one-hour drive we shared on our way to the recording studio. Our conversation during that ride revolved around the movie's central theme, the apocalypse—the end of time. In the film's dystopian vision, the world lies in ruins, and only three survivors remain, peering out from a bunker in a barren, lifeless landscape.

What followed was nothing short of magic. Upon arriving at the studio, keyboardist and arranger, Jim Blazer, joined Sputzy for a twenty-minute discussion to map out the song's structure and instrumentation. In just four hours, we recorded the track which seemed effortless. Sputzy's vocal performance was nothing less than extraordinary, capturing the emotion and weight of the moment with breathtaking clarity.

We left the studio that day with a rough mix of the song in hand, and with a strong sense that we had created something special. When I eventually record the audio version of this book, *'If Tomorrow Comes'* will most certainly be included. Given the global tension and uncertainty in the world today, the song's title feels timelier, and more haunting than ever. *If Tomorrow Comes...*

One Heart...One Love

Book One - Closing Statement & Looking Ahead to Book Two

It's uncommon for an author to step back and reflect on their own journey within the closing pages of a book. Writing this book has been a valuable experience, one that not only recalled significant moments but also addressed past disappointments and provided insights into the lessons offered by my first written journey in the music business.

Looking back, I now understand that failure isn't merely an obstacle; it's a critical component in the formula for growth and eventual success. The music industry is, at its core, a relentless, unpredictable arena where overnight success is more myth than reality. Behind every chart-topping single and every star whose name lights up a marquee lies a backstory woven with persistence, missteps, bold reinventions, and countless hours spent honing their craft. Fame may seem instantaneous, but its roots run deep, planted long before the spotlight ever finds its mark. And even then, no amount of talent, grit, or impeccable timing can truly guarantee success.

I've also come to recognize that the music business is less a well-oiled machine and more a fragile, ever-shifting ecosystem. It's a complex, high-stakes collaboration where a single misstep, or stroke of luck, can alter the trajectory of an entire project. If only making hit records were as simple as gardening: enriching the soil, providing water and sunshine, sowing the finest seeds, and you can almost count on a bountiful harvest. But in this business, even when the ingredients are seemingly perfect, a phenomenal song, a visionary producer, powerful promotion, strong media buzz, and a razor-sharp marketing plan, the odds of hitting the charts can still be slim to none. After all, peppers and tomatoes don't have to compete for airplay or Billboard rankings.

Looking ahead, I'm excited to begin the second book of this ongoing story: Music Business Stories – Book Two: 1986 to 2000. Planned for a Fall 2026 release.

Stories In Book Two will include:

* Recording trips in 1986 to Jamaica and adventures at Hedonism II. Recording Chokey Taylor and the S.W.A.M.P. Band at Tuff Gong recording studios in Kingston and flying adventures between Negril and Kingston.

*Behind the scenes stories of the artists and the launching and co-publishing the Los Angeles based, nationally distributed, Bi-Weekly Trade Magazine, The R&B Report. 1987 – 1991. All hands on deck – with Billly Bass, Graham Armstrong, Tookie Dileo, Joe Isgro, and the publication staff Based on the West Coast

In the early 1990s Nile Rodgers and Tom Cossie formed ROCO Entertainment and Ear Candy Records. They established office space and a recording studio in New York City, and introduced their label at BMG's global presidents meeting at the Algarve in Portugal.

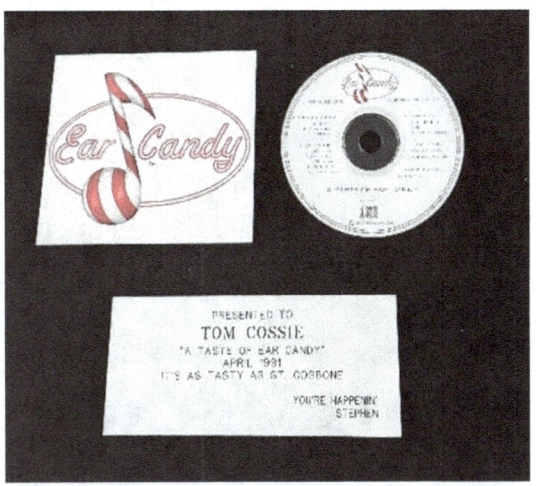

*While working with Ear Candy, the story continued; I interviewed with Donald Trump to become president of his new record label, Trump Records. The interview focused on the label's direction. When a friend later asked about my impression of Trump, I replied, "If you know the business policies of Roy Cohn, you know Donald Trump."

*An overview of the venture capital investment journey with Dormont Technology, including the development and launch of StarTracker™ software—a comprehensive "Record Company System in a Box" as recognized by the industry.

This period was marked by unique challenges in the software industry during the dot-com bust.

*Financing software through unconventional means; The development of StarTracker in exchange for two 328 GTS Ferrari sports cars and a record contract for the software development team's band.

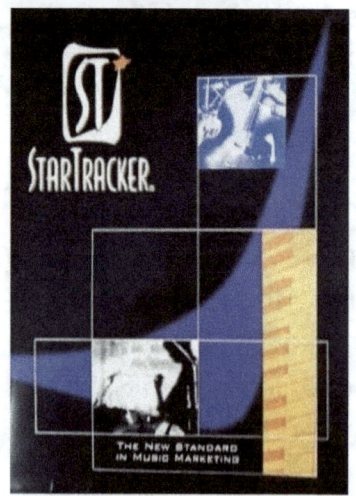

*Saturn Records resumes operations with national independent distribution and establishes BMI and ASCAP publishing companies.

Street Stuff Music Inc.

*   St. Cosbone Winery – Music and Bachus

* Cossie Photo- www.cossiephoto.com and the transition into the Healthcare Profession.

Stories in Book Three will Include

Book Three commences at the turn of the century, encompassing the years 2000 through 2025. It documents the formation of a music publishing partnership with Vito DiSalvo's Mifflin Hills Music, as well as a professional transition into the healthcare sector via an appointment as Vice President of Real Estate Development and Government Relations at Vantage Health Care. The narrative highlights the establishment of Cossie Photo, illustrating experience as a photojournalist in Washington, DC on Capitol Hill for The Vantage Healthcare Group of Hospitals. Additionally, Book Three contains accounts from photo sessions in New York City with world wrestling champion Bruno Samartino and his flamboyant legal representative, Marty Lazzaro. Scenes from NYC, The Feast of San Gennaro

Triple H, Bruno, Marty & Cos at Umberto's Clam House

By the mid-2020s, the story culminates in the founding of Surman Gardens, a boutique sauce company, and the launch of the Tomic "Taste Heat" Jam and BBQ Sauces brand. The anticipated release date for Book Three is 2027.

Street Stuff Music, Inc.

14661 Jetport Loop, Suite 180, Ft. Myers, FL 33913

www.streetstuffmusic.com

For more information about the author, products and services
go to - www.streetstuffmusic.com

www.ingramcontent.com/pod-product-compliance
Lightning Source LLC
Chambersburg PA
CBHW070547130626
46556CB00001B/54